# MEETING EXCELLENCE

# MEETING EXCELLENCE

## 33 TOOLS TO LEAD MEETINGS
## THAT GET RESULTS

Glenn Parker

Robert Hoffman

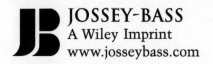

JOSSEY-BASS
A Wiley Imprint
www.josseybass.com

Published by Jossey-Bass
A Wiley Imprint
989 Market Street, San Francisco, CA 94103-1741    www.josseybass.com

Jossey-Bass books and products are available through most bookstores. To contact Jossey-Bass directly call
our Customer Care Department within the U.S. at 800-956-7739, outside the U.S. at 317-572-3986, or
fax 317-572-4002.

Jossey-Bass also publishes its books in a variety of electronic formats. Some content that appears in print may
not be available in electronic books.

**Library of Congress Cataloging-in-Publication Data**
Parker, Glenn M., 1938-
    Meeting excellence : 33 tools to lead meetings that get results / by Glenn Parker, Robert Hoffman.
        p. cm.
    Includes bibliographical references and index.
    ISBN-13: 978-0-7879-8281-2 (alk. paper)
    ISBN-10: 0-7879-8281-4 (alk. paper)
        1. Business meetings—Handbooks, manuals, etc.  I. Hoffman, Robert, 1958-  II. Title.
    HF5734.5.P35 2006
    658.4'56—dc22                                                        2005028347

Printed in the United States of America
FIRST EDITION
*HB Printing*   10 9 8 7 6 5 4 3 2 1

# CONTENTS

## PART 3

## CLOSING AND FOLLOWING UP ON THE MEETING

## PART 4

## RESOURCES

When we began thinking about preparing a series of tools for improving the quality of meetings at the Novartis Oncology Business Unit, we had no plans to put together a book on the subject. Our mission was to create a series of brief, user-friendly documents for people who plan and lead meetings at all levels in the organization. From Novartis employees who voiced their feelings at a number of open space and focus group meetings in both in the United States and Europe, we learned that existing meeting resources did not meet their needs.

They were ready to move beyond lists of best practices to more specific how-to job aids—that is, to something more akin to a cookbook on meeting management. For example, they already knew that cultural differences must be considered in facilitating a global meeting. What they really needed was a tool that said, here are the specific things you should avoid and encourage in order to achieve clear communication in a multicultural meeting. In other words, these meeting facilitators wanted us to drill down to the issues they face daily and then prepare tools to help them address these issues.

With encouragement and strong support of David Epstein, president of the Novartis Oncology Business Unit, Glenn was brought into the organization to work with Bob to collect additional data by observing team meetings, examining existing meeting documents, and conducting a number of intensive individual interviews. The outcome of this assessment was a comprehensive change effort that came to be known as the Meeting Excellence program. This effort includes a range of options for people leading meetings within Novartis:

1. *Web-Based Tools.* All the Meeting Excellence tools are posted on the Novartis intranet, where they can be accessed and downloaded by employees.

2. *Facilitation Skills Workshop.* A one-day development program that focuses on 15 behaviors of a successful facilitator and includes intensive skill practice role-plays using company-specific scenarios.

3. *Meeting Assessment Survey.* A 36-item survey that measures the effectiveness of the meetings of a specific team. The team leader gets a summary of the results and advice on how to facilitate an action-planning session with team members.

4. *Observation* and *Feedback.* A trained observer attends a team meeting, takes notes, and provides the leader with feedback designed to reinforce the 15 behaviors of a successful facilitator.

5. *Coaching.* An outside person works with team leaders individually over time to help upgrade their meeting facilitation skills.

## Background and Purpose of the Book

When it became clear that the tools developed for Novartis Oncology had wide applicability and would be useful to other organizations, the idea for a book surfaced in our thinking. People from other organizations called with requests to see and perhaps use the materials. At that point it became obvious that a book provided the best way to make these tools available to people in other organizations who were searching for practical advice and tools for more effective meeting management. At the same time, everyone also seemed to be saying that team leaders had little time to wade through long documents to find specific tips, techniques, and samples that they could use in the meeting scheduled for next week.

*Meeting Excellence* provides a wide variety of ready-to-use tools that have been tested by team leaders and facilitators in a variety of organizational settings around the world. In this book you will find answers to questions frequently asked about meetings:

I know that good planning makes for a great meeting, but what specifically should I do before my next meeting?

My meetings always have an agenda but it does not seem to help very much; what can I do to improve the effectiveness of my agendas?

As a leader of a new team, what should I include in my kick-off meeting next week?

I lead a virtual team that includes people from six different countries; what are some ways I can ensure everyone participates in our discussions?

What are ways I can deal with disruptive people who talk too long and often, and with the ones who do other work during the meeting?

We have a lot of presentations at our meetings and most are dull and boring; what can I do to change that?

As a new leader of an old team, I have noticed what seems to be a lack of trust on the part of certain members toward other members; can anything be done to develop a climate of trust on a team?

Although I have a good action agenda, we always seem to go off on a tangent and then not accomplish all the items on the agenda or just rush through them at the end of the meeting; can I do anything about this?

When people look like they are not interested or have a question but say nothing, is there anything I can do to get them involved?

In most of my meetings a few people do most of the talking while the large majority sit quietly most of the time; since we seem to get all the agenda items completed, should I worry about this lack of participation?

The meetings of the ongoing team that I lead have become very dull and boring; can I do anything to make them more fun and livelier?

How do I close a meeting on a positive note when people are anxious to leave?

What do I do about people who agree to take responsibility for action items but then do not complete them on time?

How do I deal with the fact that certain decisions made at our meeting do not get communicated back to line management or do not get communicated accurately?

I know it is a good idea to evaluate our meetings, but people are impatient to leave and do not want to take the time to fill out a form; what should I do?

## Audience for This Book

We wrote this book for people in organizations who spend increasing amounts of their time in meetings. As organizational development and team building professionals we often hear comments from employees expressing their frustration and dissatisfaction with teamwork. In fact, their frustration can usually be traced to their association of teamwork with team meetings. In their world, since meetings are bad, teams must be a bad idea. They conclude that the organization is wasting its time and resources pursuing a strategy that has teams as its centerpiece.

When you pierce the outer layer of frustration you find a great deal of time being spent in meetings that are poorly planned and poorly implemented, with little or no positive outcome. And so we decided to do something about it by drawing on our experience to provide tools for achieving effective meetings that are both brief and practical. People told us the tools need to be brief because they do not have the time to wade through long documents to get what they need. And they told us the tools need to be practical because they do not need to be told again about the importance of effective meeting management and they do not need to know the theory that underlies it. In that context the tools in this book provide help for a varied audience.

*Executives and high-level managers* in both the private and public sectors conduct board meetings, project review meetings, shareholder meetings, and a variety of other meetings that are critical to the success of the total organization. In many ways senior management (and the administrative staff who provide meeting support) sets the tone for the whole organization by being role models for what is expected from everyone else. People often attend and make presentations at meetings conducted by the management team. When those meetings are planned and carried out effectively, it is instructive for all those in attendance and the many others they are able to influence. When those meetings display the characteristics of Meeting Excellence, it sends a strong and positive message to the organization. Used judiciously, the tools of the Meeting Excellence program can help executives establish a positive meeting culture in their organization.

*Mid-level managers and supervisors* are responsible for functional and department staff meetings and often lead a variety of cross-functional teams that include people from both within and outside the company. Many of these people are stretched thin by increasing demands on their time coupled with the large number of tasks and projects for which they are held accountable. Since they often lack administrative support to help plan their meetings, they will be glad to reach for some of the Meeting Excellence tools that will make the job of planning their next meeting faster, easier, and ultimately more effective.

*Team leaders and meeting facilitators* who are out there on the front lines facing the frustration of team members who do not want to sit through another bad meeting will find among the tools of Meeting Excellence specific guidance for preparing and facilitating a meeting that will make them organizational heroes. They will find tools to help plan their next meeting, facilitate the meeting so that it accomplishes its objectives, and then follow up to ensure that the outcomes are implemented. For example, by this time most meeting leaders know they need an agenda, but *Meeting Excellence* provides specific guidance on how to prepare an effective agenda—including a template they can follow. The same is true of the more than 30 other tools included here.

*Human resource, organizational development, and team-building professionals* who are consulting with and providing training for team managers, leaders, facilitators, and members will find specific advice and tips they can use in their team-training and team-building interventions. The book also includes many surveys and checklists they can use to diagnose a team, assess a team leader, or conduct a needs assessment as part of their consulting services to the organization.

## Overview of the Contents

The tools in *Meeting Excellence* are grouped and presented according to the three phases of a meeting:

1.  Preparing for the Meeting
2.  Facilitating the Meeting
3.  Closing and Following Up on the Meeting

The Resources section at the end includes a variety of other information and tools designed to supplement the contents of *Meeting Excellence*.

The key to a successful meeting is rooted in all the work you do before the start of the meeting. In fact, it is very difficult, perhaps impossible, to overcome lack of planning and preparation once the meeting has begun. Therefore, in Part 1 you will find tools that will help you

- Decide if your next meeting is really necessary.

- Determine what needs to be done to prepare yourself and the team.

- Prepare an agenda.

- Define team meeting roles.

- Integrate a new member on to your team.

- Deal with the departure of a team member.

- Create your team's ground rules.

- Plan a new team kick-off meeting.

- Design and facilitate a team off-site meeting.

- Decide how to open the meeting on a positive note.

- Write clear e-mail messages.

Now think about the time after the meeting has begun. You are faced with the task of accomplishing your meeting objectives in the face of a variety of obstacles. In Part 2 you will find tools designed to

- Manage the time during the meeting.
- Stay on track and focused on your planned outcomes.
- Facilitate effective participation in your meeting.
- Build a climate of trust in your meeting.
- Facilitate a videoconference meeting.
- Facilitate a teleconference meeting.
- Ensure clear communication in a multicultural meeting.
- Make an effective decision.
- Help everyone deliver an effective presentation in a team meeting.
- Resolve conflicts that may arise in your meeting.
- Understand and respond to nonverbal behavior.
- Deal with difficult behavior in your meeting.
- Have fun while you get the work done in the meeting.
- Plan refreshments that will be genuinely refreshing.

Every meeting should have a strong closing. And there is still much work to do after the meeting to ensure that agreements are implemented. Part 3 provides tools to help you

- Close a meeting on a positive and forward-looking note.
- Evaluate your meeting with a two-minute drill, a five-minute activity, and a ten-minute assessment.
- Create a set of brief but effective meeting notes.
- Create action items that get action.
- Follow up on the meeting effectively.
- Facilitate external communication with key stakeholders.

The book ends with a Resources section that includes

- A review of the effectiveness of current Web-based meeting tools. Since this field is changing rapidly, it is important to use the information here as a starting point for your search for the best Web-based tool for your team.

- An article titled "The Seven Sins of Deadly Meetings" that provides both a description of common meeting problems and suggestions for overcoming each problem.

- A self-assessment tool for team members that provides an opportunity for members to evaluate their role as a meeting participant.

- Ten case problems that you can use to facilitate a discussion or conduct a training session on meetings.

- A quiz to test yourself and your teammates on Meeting Excellence.

- An annotated bibliography of books, articles, Web sites, and videos that we have found to be helpful.

## Acknowledgments

We would like to thank a number of our colleagues at Novartis Oncology who provided support, encouragement, advice, and specific feedback on the tools. Although many people contributed, we would especially like to acknowledge David Epstein, Michele Galen, Elizabeth Kearns, Jim Jaffee, Steve Goldfarb, Carrie Kifner, and Catherine Sadler. In addition, Diana Morris, an external communications consultant, helped us create the concept of Meeting Excellence.

Glenn would like to thank his wife, Judy, for her support during the development of this project and for just about everything else of importance in his life. He would like to thank his children, Michael, Jill, and Ellen, and his grandchildren, Drew, Emily, Max, and Jake for bringing much joy and laughter into his life.

Bob would like to thank his wife, Deanna, for her love, her laughter, and her faith in him and their marriage. Bob would also like to thank his children—Sarah, Christopher, Melissa, and Rachel—for reminding him about what is really important in life. Finally, Bob would like to acknowledge his father, Marshall, and his mother, Ann, who passed away during the publication of this book and without whose guidance, love, and support he would not be the man he is today.

*November 2005*

Glenn Parker
*Skillman, New Jersey*

Robert Hoffman
*Watchung, New Jersey*

PART I

# PREPARING FOR THE MEETING

# 1

# IS THIS MEETING NECESSARY?

## Purpose

Too often, people get caught up in thinking, "We always have a project meeting Tuesday morning at 10," or "We haven't gotten the group together for a while," or similar rationalizations for having a team meeting. Yet sometimes, deciding *not* to meet may be the best use of everyone's valuable time.

### Key Questions to Ask Up Front

- *Is there a clear purpose for the meeting?* "Developing a plan for responding to issues raised by the site investigator" is a clear purpose for a problem-solving meeting. However, for "Reviewing reports from sites," a meeting may not be what you need at all.

- *Should we meet now?* It may be best to postpone the meeting if required information is missing, a critical member who should be present to explain a vital issue is not available, or an important organizational change is about to be announced.

- *Is there a better alternative?* If the purpose of the meeting is to communicate information such as status updates, it may be more efficient and just as effective to use an appropriate electronic method. Consider sending e-mail with an attachment or posting the information on the team space. If the purpose of the meeting involves only two or three members, perhaps an informal subgroup session would be a better alternative. If the purpose involves information gathering from some members, one-to-one meetings or telephone conversations with these individuals may be a preferred method.

- *What if the meeting is not held?* What would not be accomplished? How would team members react? How would senior managers react?

If the answers are "Nothing would be missed" or "There would be a loud cheer throughout the organization" (or both), you have your answer.

The general rule:

## No Purpose = No Meeting!

**Related Tools**

- Preparing for Your Next Meeting (tool #2)
- How to Prepare an Action Agenda (tool #3)
- Planning an Off-Site Meeting That's On Target (tool #9)

# PREPARING FOR YOUR NEXT MEETING

## *Purpose*

As the meeting facilitator, you have done your job. The meeting notice and agenda are done, the notice and necessary documents have been transmitted to the members, the meeting room and equipment have been confirmed, and the refreshments have been ordered. Your meeting preparation is complete. Or is it?

As a team member, you are ready to attend your next team meeting. You have a copy of the agenda, the related documents have been downloaded and printed, you know where the meeting will be held, and you've calculated how long it will take to arrive at the room in time for the start of the meeting. Your meeting preparation is complete. Not really.

Even though the mechanics of the meeting are set, real meeting preparation requires some additional effort. The purpose of this tool is to offer suggestions for the team leader and team members on ways to increase their effectiveness by investing in several preparation activities.

### Tips for the Meeting Facilitator

- *Decide if the meeting is necessary.* Just because your project team meets every Friday morning to review progress, do you really need to meet *this* Friday? Would everyone be better served by canceling the meeting? For more specific ideas on deciding whether to hold a team meeting, see tool #1, "Is This Meeting Necessary?"

- *Be clear about your key meeting outcome.* What is the one decision, solution, or other action that will make this a successful meeting? *Note:* We do not mean that you should have a predefined action that you want but that you are clear about the issue that needs to be addressed.

- *Review your list of invitees.* With your key meeting outcomes in hand, check the list of people invited to the meeting to ensure it includes only those people who really need to attend—the ones with the expertise needed to reach the decision or solve the problem associated with your key meeting outcome. The key players typically include

  - The relevant subject matter experts

  - The empowered decision makers

  - The significant stakeholders

  - The important implementers

Some people should not be invited. These people include

  - Members who have no interest in and nothing to contribute to any of the agenda items

  - Other people who have only a marginal interest in the issues and only sit in to observe

  - Senior managers whose presence is not necessary and may inhibit the participation of the relevant members

- *Consider the materials needed for the meeting.* What readings or handouts are necessary to support the agenda items? Will these materials be ready for communication prior to the meeting, or for distribution during the meeting if it's not appropriate to hand them out in advance?

- *Distribute the meeting notice and agenda prior to the meeting.* Your team should establish a ground rule that indicates when the agenda should be sent to the meeting participants. As a general rule, 48 hours in advance of the meeting is a minimum. However, if team members travel a great deal or the meeting often requires considerable preparation, the meeting notice and agenda may need to reach the participants earlier. For example, we know of certain high-level meetings where the agenda is distributed two weeks prior to the meeting.

- *Communicate with the key players.* If one person is scheduled to deliver the presentation that sets the stage for the essential outcome, talk with that person before the meeting. Is the presentation ready? Is the presenter aware of likely questions about the issue? Prepared to handle the questions? If someone is responsible for a report that is a critical agenda item, check to confirm that the report will be complete in time for the meeting. If any important guests are supposed to attend, provide them with an orientation that prepares them for the meeting.

- *Determine the decision-making method.* If one of the key meeting outcomes is a decision, decide how you will make the decision. What method is appropriate for this particular issue, the dynamics of the team, and the available time? See tool #19, "How to Make a Decision."

- *Identify the relevant ground rules.* Does the group need to be reminded about certain ground rules as they consider specific issues? For example, if an important decision is on the agenda, you may want to do a quick review of your team's norms regarding decision making. See tool #7, "Establishing Your Team's Ground Rules."

- *Do an attendance check.* If the involvement and support of certain people are critical, will those people attend the meeting? For example, if one of the key outcomes concerns a change in the marketing plan, then the principal marketing representative needs to be present. Therefore, it is important that you check the responses to the meeting notice to see who is planning to attend. If certain key people cannot be there, you may need to change the agenda, obtain a substitute who can act on behalf of the missing participant, or change the meeting time.

- *Complete a head count.* A related concern is the number of people scheduled to attend. If one of the meeting outcomes is consensus on an important decision, you will want the group to be small. If you want input from a wide range of people on an issue, you will want a large group of active participants. In either case (as well as other possible scenarios), knowing the number of people expected to attend will help you prepare to facilitate the meeting. For example, if 20 people are expected to attend a meeting where reaching a true consensus is important, you may wish to have only the core team present at the beginning of the meeting when the issue is discussed.

- *Anticipate problems or obstacles.* The effective facilitator is rarely surprised. The effective facilitator foresees troublesome issues and is prepared to deal with them. Do you expect an issue to be contentious? What objections can be anticipated? Who stands to lose something? Which agenda items may take longer than planned? Which agenda items can be postponed to the next meeting? What if a key player is unable to attend at the last minute?

- *Check on the meeting logistics.* Make sure the room is large enough and contains a sufficient number of chairs, the necessary meeting room equipment is ordered, the communications (audio, video, Web) are set, and, if appropriate, the refreshments are ordered.

- *Play "What-if?"* Besides following the tips about logistics, effective facilitators play a mental game of what-if scenarios prior to the meeting. For example:

  - What if a senior manager shows up?
  - What if the meeting starts 20 minutes late?
  - What if the equipment does not work?
  - What if the person responsible for the critical agenda item gets sick at the last minute and does not attend?
  - What if only half or a quarter of the expected people show up?
  - What if two key team members get into an argument?
  - What if the team makes a decision with which you strongly disagree?

## Tips for the Team Member

- *Review the agenda.* Read the agenda sufficiently in advance of the meeting to address any concerns you may have, gather any required information, obtain whatever input you may need from your manager and colleagues, or clarify your decision-making authority on key issues.

- *Prepare your positions.* If the agenda includes a critical decision, take some time to consider your position (and the position of your management) on the issue. At the same time, gather your data, review other documentation, and organize your thoughts.

- *Clarify your authority.* If the agenda specifies a decision on a critical issue, are you empowered to speak for your department? Since efficient meeting management depends on members' being empowered to make a commitment, be clear about your authority before the meeting.

- *Prepare and review your action items.* If you are responsible for tasks that are due at the meeting, complete the items. Equally important, understand the ground rules on presenting the material. Is it expected that the work will be sent out in advance of the meeting? How long in advance of the meeting must the material be sent? What format is preferred? Can you expect people to read the material or will you need to review the content at the meeting?

- *Practice your presentation.* If you are scheduled to deliver a presentation at the meeting, do a dry run. See tool #20, "Presenting at a Team Meeting."

- *Manage your schedule.* Try to avoid back-to-back meetings in different locations. Plan your time so that you can arrive at the team meeting a few minutes before the meeting begins.

**Related Tools**

- Is This Meeting Necessary? (tool #1)
- Defining Team Meeting Roles (tool #4)
- Establishing Your Team's Ground Rules (tool #7)
- Planning an Off-Site Meeting That's On Target (tool #9)
- How to Make a Decision (tool #19)
- Presenting at a Team Meeting (tool #20)
- Are You a Meeting Marvel? (resource C)
- What Would You Do? (resource D)

# HOW TO PREPARE AN ACTION AGENDA

3

## *Purpose*

The key to a successful meeting starts well before the meeting takes place, and the heart of pre-meeting planning is the creation of an action agenda. A solid action agenda drives the dynamics of the meeting toward a successful outcome. An action agenda differs from the more typical agenda (a plain list of topics to be covered) in its focus on *outcomes*.

The purpose of this tool is to outline and provide a rationale for each component of an action agenda. It also includes a sample meeting notice and agenda.

### Keys to an Action Agenda

- *Timing.* Provide a beginning and ending time for the meeting. The starting time is not enough, as members need to know when the meeting will end so they can plan the remainder of their day. *Tip:* Consider starting and ending at odd times. For example, you might begin your meeting at 9:12 A.M. rather than the more traditional 9:00 A.M. An odd starting time gets attention and it also allows members some time to leave a previous meeting and still arrive at your meeting before it starts.

- *Key meeting outcome.* Identify and highlight the one or two outcomes critical for that meeting. A key meeting outcome ensures that the energy and time of the team are properly focused. It means that even if no other issues are addressed, the meeting will be successful.

- *Pre-meeting preparation.* Most meetings involve some homework in advance. To be effective meeting contributors, members need to prepare for the meeting. Preparation may involve reading documents or presentations but it can also involve thinking about and researching a topic. Therefore, the meeting notice should indicate the required preparation activities.

- *Ranking the agenda items.* Always list agenda items in order of their importance. The first item is the most important and is usually associated with the key meeting outcome. The obvious rationale for rank order by importance is that it ensures that the most important items get considered, get considered when the energy of the members is highest, and, if necessary, get additional time to fully explore the issue. *One exception:* some teams use the first few minutes of a meeting to clear away any administrative items. This can be productive, but be careful to ration administration carefully or it will crowd out substantive matters.

- *Be specific.* The topics selected for the agenda should be as specific as possible. For example, rather than "Update on B-47," it is more helpful to say "Determine the next steps of the B-47 marketing plan." In addition to specificity, all agenda items should be stated in terms of an outcome or objective. In other words: What do we need to accomplish to satisfactorily complete the agenda item?

- *How long will it take?* Another useful technique is to include an estimate of the time necessary to complete each item. As a planning tool, this will help determine if the number of agenda items is appropriate for time set aside for the meeting. The result may be a need to revise the agenda or the length of the meeting. It is clearly an *estimate* of the time. During the meeting it gives the meeting facilitator some options. For example, as you approach the end of the time allocated to an agenda item, the facilitator can ask the team if they wish to continue, move the item to the next meeting, or ask a subgroup to handle it. Each of the options has consequences, but the question places the decision in the hands of the members.

- *What action will we take?* Although the outcome statement should make the objective clear, it is useful to clearly state what action is necessary on the agenda item. Is the goal to inform, make a decision, agree on a plan, or develop a strategy?

- *Who is responsible?* Someone—either a member or a guest—should own each agenda item. It is the responsible person's role to prepare and provide the materials, present the information, answer questions, and be a resource. Sometimes the issue owner also facilitates the discussion. One benchmark of a successful meeting is the sharing of responsibility for meeting effectiveness.

- *Who's invited to the party?* The meeting notice will specify the people who are asked to attend. In the case of an intact team, the attendance list is predetermined. However, many meetings need an attendance list based on the purpose of the meeting. Here are some criteria for determining who should attend:

    - Needs the information to get the task done or to understand the big picture.

    - Manages an area that will be affected by the decision.

    - Will be involved later.

    - Has the facts or information needed.

    - Is in charge of the project or will have to implement the decision.

    - Is the decision maker.

Some teams use the option of categorizing the invitations into two categories:

> *Required:* Your presence is necessary to achieve the key outcome or agenda item.

> *Optional:* You may wish to attend to learn more about the subject or how the group operates.

## SAMPLE MEETING NOTICE AND AGENDA

Name of Team, Board, or Group: Blander Project Team

Date of Meeting: December 3

Time: 10:25 A.M. to 11:59 A.M.

Venues: Milan Meeting Room: Como 203; U.S. Meeting Room: Madison 102

Dial-in Number: 877-555-1234

Pin Codes: Host: 5551234; Others: 10011

Key Meeting Outcome: A plan to deal with the imperfections in the package design.

Pre-Meeting Preparation: Review the notes of the previous meeting; read the attached documents; read and comment on the publications to be reviewed; develop your thoughts on ways to deal with the imperfections in the package design.

## AGENDA

| Topic/Outcome | Time | Action | Person Responsible |
|---|---|---|---|
| 1. Determine the steps of an action plan to deal with the imperfections in the package design | 30 min. | Decision on a plan | Manuel |
| 2. Define an action plan to address recommendations submitted by the task force | 15 min. | Decision on a plan | John & Hans |
| 3. Define a action plan to address the relationship with the Marketing consultant | 15 min. | Decision on a plan | John & Hans |
| 4. Acceptance of the Blander product plan | 10 min. | Decision | All |
| 5. Feedback on the management report | 20 min. | Approval or rejection | All |

All attachments are stored in the Blander Team Space.

**Related Tools**

- Preparing for Your Next Meeting (tool #2)
- Components of a New Team Kick-Off Meeting (tool #8)
- Planning an Off-Site Meeting That's On Target (tool #9)

# DEFINING TEAM MEETING ROLES

## *Purpose*

The leader leads. The facilitator facilitates. The scribe takes notes. It seems rather simple. Does anything else need to be said about team role clarification?

Well, yes. The leader leads—but sometimes the leader also facilitates and even takes notes. It can get confusing. When there is confusion on a team, sometimes things do not get done or they get done poorly. In our fast-paced, challenging world, we cannot afford role ambiguity and its negative effects.

The purpose of this tool is to clarify the various team roles, including the potential areas of overlap and confusion. It should also be mentioned that many teams incorporate a delineation of team roles in their team charter as a way of minimizing the dangers of role ambiguity. We expect that many teams will use the material in the tool as a starting point for that section of their charter.

In this tool we are focusing only on the responsibilities of each role in a team meeting—not the total role, which may include responsibilities beyond the scope of a meeting. The leader, of course, has many responsibilities other than leading team meetings.

These are the four most important team roles:

- Team leader
- Facilitator
- Scribe
- Meeting participant

This tool draws heavily on material found in G. Parker, *Team Depot: A Warehouse of Over 585 Tools to Rejuvenate Your Team,* San Francisco: Jossey-Bass, 2002.

Some teams also identify two other helpful roles:

- Timekeeper
- Parking lot attendant

## Defining Team Meeting Roles

- *Team leader.* The leader's main responsibilities include ensuring that the group stays focused on the key meeting outcomes, the overall goals of the team, and the organizational context of the team's goals, as well as providing relevant scientific, technical, and corporate policy information and highlighting the importance of building effective external relationships. When someone other than the leader plays the role of meeting facilitator, the team leader concentrates on providing scientific, technical, and corporate information while the facilitator provides the group process leadership and helps people stay focused on the matter at hand.

- *Meeting facilitator.* The facilitator manages the process side of the meeting with tools such as active listening, various types of questions, and reading nonverbal cues. In many cases the leader also serves as the meeting facilitator, making the job all the more difficult. In other cases, an outside process expert or another team member plays the role of facilitator.

- *Scribe.* Sometimes referred to as the recorder, secretary, or project administrator, this person is responsible for capturing the key meeting outcomes. We refer to the resulting document as *notes* rather than *minutes,* since the latter term implies a detailed record of everything that takes place similar to a transcript. The term *notes* has come to mean a record of the meeting highlights. See tool #30 ("Meeting Notes: Capturing the Essence of Your Meeting"). Teams may have different ground rules for their meeting notes but typically they include the following:

- All decisions made at the meeting.
- A list of all new and outstanding action items.
- Date, time, and location of the next meeting as well as any agenda items that are known at the time.
- Members and guests present at the meeting.
- Other highlights

- *Timekeeper.* The timekeeper helps the team stay on track by making everyone aware of time. The timekeeper knows the time allocated for each agenda item and will let the leader or facilitator (and the presenter, if any) know when the limit is about to be reached on an item. The leader or facilitator can also serve as timekeeper, but it is usually better to ask another member to handle this task.

- *Parking lot attendant.* This is a very useful role for helping the team stay on track and focused on the agenda. When the team drifts off the agenda topic to discuss another issue, the leader can suggest that the issue be placed in the "parking lot." The attendant records the item for inclusion in the notes and as a possible agenda item at a future meeting. At the end of the meeting, the parking lot attendant reports the issues.

- *Meeting participant.* The various meeting leadership roles demand so much attention that it is easy to forget the large group of other meeting participants, who play a powerful role in shaping the success of a team meeting. Responsibilities of meeting participants include
  - *Prepare for the meeting.* Review the agenda, note your responsibilities on the agenda, get ready to discuss and decide the relevant items (consulting with your manager as needed), read the required materials, and complete your action items.
  - *Make appropriate arrangements if you are unable to attend.* Inform the team leader as soon as possible, submit your action items to

the leader and, if possible, identify and orient a substitute to represent you at the meeting.

◆ *Be on time.* In fact, it is better to arrive early, so as to have a few minutes to talk with your teammates and get focused on this meeting.

◆ *Participate.* Ask questions, seek clarification, offer opinions, share your expertise, challenge assumptions, listen actively with an open mind, and help resolve differences and achieve a consensus on key issues.

◆ *Take notes.* Do not wait for or rely on the meeting notes—you want to be ready to get started on your action items as well as report to your manager and colleagues. Use the agenda as your outline for taking notes. Jot down all decisions and relevant action items.

◆ *Help the leader or facilitator.* Think of the meeting as *your* meeting because it really is your meeting, too. You want the meeting to be successful as well as an effective use of your time. So help the team stay on track, follow the agenda, and manage the time. You can also help the leader get others involved by asking questions, by looking for common ground when differences arise, and by summarizing key ideas and reaching a consensus.

◆ *Avoid being a problem.* Don't monopolize the discussion, engage in side conversation, be unnecessarily argumentative, attack other members, or do other work during the meeting. Turn off your cell phone, beeper, and other electronic devices, and don't play with your PDA.

## Related Tools

- Preparing for Your Next Meeting (tool #2)
- Meeting Time Management (tool #12)

- Staying on Track (tool #13)
- How to Get Effective Participation (tool #14)
- How to Make a Decision (tool #19)
- Managing Meeting Monsters (tool #23)
- Meeting Notes (tool #30)
- Are You a Meeting Marvel? (resource C)

# 5

# HOW TO INTEGRATE A NEW MEMBER

## *Purpose*

Turnover among team members is inevitable. A new employee joins the company and is assigned to your team. A long-time member of your team is reassigned to a new project and replaced by another person from that department. Membership change is expected in the natural history of a team.

However, a new person attending a team meeting can slow team progress by expecting answers to questions explored in depth months ago and disrupt group dynamics by violating long-standing team ground rules. Alternatively, a new member can bring needed expertise, a fresh look at the issues, and some spice to a team's dreary meeting process. The key to the successful integration of new member is thoughtful planning.

The purpose of this tool is to provide ideas for both the team leader and the new member that will smooth the transition and minimize the integration problems. See also tool #6, "When a Member Leaves the Team."

### Tips for the Team Leader

- Welcome the new person, preferably in a face-to-face meeting, but at least in a telephone conversation if it's not possible to get together.

  - At this meeting, provide your perspective on the team, including critical issues, upcoming challenges, and your expectations as a leader.

  - Discuss the new member's concerns and questions about the team. Ask, "How do you see yourself helping the team achieve its goals?"

- Get to know something about the person's life outside of work (family, hobbies, and interests) by sharing similar things about yourself.

- Provide the relevant documents and information—including the project plan, team charter, ground rules, and access to databases.

- Assign another member of the team to serve as a mentor, sharing a personal perspective on the team and generally helping the new person understand the project, the culture, and the politics of the team.

- Send the team a message about the new member, including a photo if possible. Explain something about the new member's background and what role the person will play on the team.

- When someone is joining the team to replace a current team member, ask the outgoing member to brief the new one about the team and any issues that are relevant to their role. If possible, ask the current team member to stay on for a month to smooth the transition.

- Ask the new member to meet as many other members as possible either face-to-face or by telephone. The mentor may facilitate some of these meetings.

- If team training is available, encourage the new member to participate.

- At the next team meeting, ask the mentor to introduce the new member. Then ask the new member to provide a perspective on how they plan to help the team.

- As soon as possible, get the new person working on a task, action item, or subteam.

- If the person is new to the company, provide an orientation to the relevant organizational structure and decision-making bodies.

- You may wish to have an exit interview with the departing member to ask for feedback on the team, your leadership style, and ways to help both the new member and the overall team succeed.

## Tips for the New Member

- Ask the current member you are replacing for views of the team and suggestions for how you can succeed and help the team be successful.

- Meet with the team leader to share your questions and concerns about joining the team and to get the team leader's perspective on it.

- Carefully review the relevant team documents and develop a list of questions about them. Ask the team leader, current team member, your mentor, or other team members to provide the answers.

- Meet as many of your new teammates as possible, preferably in person but by phone if necessary. Ask how you can help the team.

- In advance of your first team meeting, prepare a brief statement of introduction about yourself, including both your relevant work history and personal life. Get together with the team leader or mentor to coordinate your introductions.

- Take notes at the first team meeting on issues, facts, and terminology you do not understand. After the meeting, ask the leader, your mentor, or other members to provide clarification.

- If team training is available, participate as soon as possible.

- Volunteer for an action item or to join a subteam where you believe you can make an immediate contribution.

## Related Tools

- Preparing for Your Next Meeting (tool #2)
- When a Member Leaves the Team (tool #6)
- Are You a Meeting Marvel? (resource C)

# 6

# WHEN A MEMBER LEAVES THE TEAM

## *Purpose*

People leave a team for all sorts of reasons:

> Involuntarily reassigned to another team.
>
> Volunteered for a new team assignment.
>
> Transferred to a different department.
>
> Dropped because of performance problems.
>
> Left the company.
>
> Had expertise not needed in the next phase of a project.
>
> Promoted to management.

In all cases it is important to address the impact of the departure on the team. The loss of a team member can affect two areas critical to team success:

- The skills, knowledge, and experience required to fulfill the team's mission.
- The team culture, interpersonal relationships, and meeting dynamics.

In some situations, especially those that involve a long-standing team member, it is also important to address the feelings of both the person who is leaving and the team members who remain.

The purpose of this tool is to provide suggestions to facilitate a smooth and positive departure. We look at the issue from the perspective of both the team leader and the departing member.

**Tips for the Team Leader**

- Where possible, ask the departing member and the replacement to get together for an orientation to the team, including the goals, roles, and interpersonal relationships. See tool #5. "How to Integrate a New Member."

- If, as sometimes happens, no replacement is immediately available, prepare to discuss with the team how the required work will get done.

  - Can an existing team member step in and pick up the necessary tasks?

  - Can we get temporary help in the form of a short-term reassignment or contractor?

  - Can our timeline and deliverables be revised?

- If possible, ask the departing member to stay on the team as an informal member to smooth the transition for the new member.

- At the departing member's last meeting, acknowledge the person's contributions to the team.

  - Mention their skills, knowledge, and experience, including the unique things about their personality ("subtle sense of humor," "crazy soccer fan"). Try to including some memorable event in the history of the team ("worked all night in the office to complete that project plan on time").

  - Ask other members to provide their thoughts about the person.

  - Finally, ask the departing member to speak, sharing a perspective on the team, project, and relationships with the other members.

- Where appropriate, send a personal note (not an e-mail message) expressing your feelings about the departing member's contribution to the team.

- If the departing member represents a department or function, talk with that department manager.

- ◆ Discuss the type of expertise currently needed by the team as well as the personality style of the person that makes the best fit given the culture of the team.

- ◆ Try to have some influence on the decision to replace the departing member.

- ◆ Don't forget to provide your assessment of the departing member.

- Meet with the departing member privately or by telephone for an exit interview. This is not really an interview but rather an informal discussion designed to solicit feedback on the team, the project, the team meetings, and your leadership style. This is a great opportunity to obtain an honest assessment of your team meetings and suggestions for ways to improve the meetings.

## Tips for the Departing Member

- As soon as you know you will be leaving the team, inform the team leader. Include as much information as you know about when you will leave and if a replacement has been identified.

- Prior to your final team meeting, prepare a brief, informal statement outlining your feelings about leaving the team, the project, and your teammates. Thank the members and mention any memorable events that happened during your time with the team ("that six-hour, non-stop meeting with the government agency in Japan").

- Where possible, provide your replacement with an orientation to the team, including the project, the culture, and the politics. Identify ways the new member can help the team reach its goals. Provide the person with all relevant documents.

- Where possible, stay on as an informal member of the team until the next team meeting to provide a smooth transition for the new member.

- If you represent a department or function on the team, meet with your manager to discuss your replacement on the team. Provide the manager with an update that specifically focuses on the type of person currently needed by the team.

- Meet with the team leader for an informal exit interview. Provide the leader with your assessment of the team, the project, the team meetings, and the leader's approach to the team, along with your recommendations for improvement.

### Related Tools

- Preparing for Your Next Meeting (tool #2)

- How to Integrate a New Member (tool #5)

- Managing External Communications (tool #33)

- Are You a Meeting Marvel? (resource C)

# 7

# ESTABLISHING YOUR TEAM'S GROUND RULES

## *Purpose*

Ground rules or norms are the rules of the road for team members. Norms are standards of behavior a team *expects* of its members. In practical terms, norms say: "If you are a member of this team, this is what we expect of you."

Norms serve two purposes:

- They shape and guide the actions of team members.
- They provide a standard against which members can give each other feedback.

This tool provides a list of sample ground rules designed to help your team develop its own list of "standards to live by" through discussion and consensus. Note that ground rules or norms are always written from the member's point of view.

We have also included a process for creating norms for your team. The method used to create a set of ground rules is almost as important as the rules themselves. It's important to ensure that the ground rules are embraced by all members of the team. For that to happen, the key is involving the members in the development and then the approval of a final list of rules.

The tool concludes with some suggestions for committing to and then living the norms.

## Sample Team Ground Rules

As a member of this team I will

- ❑ Show up on time for all team meetings.

- ❑ Inform the team leader when I am unable to attend a meeting (or complete an action item) as soon as I know of the problem.

- ❑ Provide the team leader with my completed action items before the meeting if I am unable to attend the meeting.

- ❑ Identify and orient an appropriate substitute if I am unable to attend.

- ❑ Read the agenda and come prepared to discuss the topics, and if necessary, be empowered to make commitments for my area or function.

- ❑ Be brief and to the point with my questions and comments.

- ❑ Ask questions when I do not understand a point.

- ❑ Listen actively to my teammates without interrupting others.

- ❑ Encourage other members to participate in team discussions and decision making.

- ❑ Work toward a real consensus by looking at both sides of an issue and changing my position when appropriate.

- ❑ Be willing to support a team consensus even if I initially do not agree with it.

- ❑ Not push my ideas on the team after a consensus has been reached.

- ❑ Not work behind the scenes to undermine a team decision after a consensus has been reached.

- ❑ Communicate honestly with my teammates, including providing realistic deliverables, due dates, action items, and status assessments.

- ❑ Remain focused on team issues rather than engaging in other work during meetings.

## Suggested Process for Developing Team Ground Rules

1. At a team meeting (preferably a face-to-face meeting), provide some background on the purpose and format of ground rules. You may also wish to present some sample ground rules to give members the flavor and format. You may draw upon the material in the "Purpose" and "Sample Team Ground Rules" sections of this tool.

2. Facilitate a brainstorming session where members toss out ideas that are posted on a flip chart or screen.

3. Reduce the list by eliminating duplicates and combining similar items.

4. Reach a tentative consensus on a list of ground rules.

5. Ask a few members of the team to review the list and edit the wording to conform to the format in the "Sample Team Ground Rules" box. Send the edited list out to the team.

6. Review and discuss the list at a subsequent meeting.

7. Reach a consensus on the final list.

## Keeping the Ground Rules in the Foreground

- Post the ground rules on the team space in a prominent place.

- Prepare several posters of the list and bring them to team meetings.

- Include the list in every meeting notice.

- Once a year, review and assess the list and make changes as needed.

## Living the Norms

- If a member goes out of the way to make sure norm is followed, acknowledge the action with something like, "Hector, thanks for sending in that report even though you were going to be on vacation when the meeting was scheduled."

- If a norm is being *consistently* violated, it is useful to point this out by saying something like, "I know you are all very interested in this issue, but we're doing a lot of interrupting and not allowing people to finish their thoughts. As a result, we're not following our ground rule on meeting discussions, and this is causing a breakdown in communication."

**Related Tools**

- Communicating in a Videoconference (tool #16)
- Teleconference Tips (tool #17)
- Achieving Clear Communication in a Multicultural Meeting (tool #18)
- How to Make a Decision (tool #19)
- Resolving Conflicts in a Team Meeting (tool #21)
- Managing Meeting Monsters (tool #23)
- Are You a Meeting Marvel? (resource C)

# 8

# COMPONENTS OF A NEW TEAM KICK-OFF MEETING

## *Purpose*

Consider these axioms:

- "You never get a second chance to make a first impression."
- "The way you start is an excellent predictor of how you will end."
- "First impressions last longer than first loves."

All axioms are generalizations. And all generalizations are subject to exceptions. However, it is still fair to say that the first team experience is critical to team success. More specifically, the first team meeting sets the tone for future meetings and is a powerful factor in establishing the team culture. As a result, it is important to both schedule a kick-off meeting and plan it carefully to achieve the desired outcomes and begin the team on a positive note.

We define a kick-off meeting as something distinctly different from simply the first meeting of a new team. A kick-off meeting is a purposeful event that provides members with an overview of the project, clarification of management's expectations, and an opportunity to raise questions and concerns, get to know their teammates, and participate in the creation of the team charter.

The purpose of this tool is to describe the components of an effective kick-off meeting. In addition, the tool includes a sample agenda for such a meeting. Circumstances may dictate some variations, but the initial meeting of a new team should include the elements described here.

**Components of a Kick-Off Meeting**

- *Project overview.* The team leader should present a few slides that give members a general understanding of why the team was formed, the overarching goals, time line, any constraints or limitations, and the role of the members. This is also a good time to discuss your leadership style as well any expectations you may have of the team.

- *Management's expectations of the team.* If possible, the sponsor or relevant member of the management team should present management's view of the team, including any specific expectations and known limitations. Issues that may be addressed here include due dates, deliverables, priorities, and the availability of resources.

- *Members' concerns and questions.* In this part of the meeting, members are asked to express any concerns and ask any questions they have about the team, management's expectations, and their own role. Issues that may come up include things like these:

  - I am already on four other teams that require 120 percent of my time. What gets priority?

  - Will we be able to get additional staff resources to meet a critical deadline?

  - It looks like the team does not include someone from the [other relevant] area. How do we compensate for that?

  - My manager just gave me a high-priority assignment that involves a major time commitment and lots of travel. How do I handle this assignment and, at the same time, manage my team responsibilities?

The leader and the senior manager should answer the questions and address the concerns. If you suspect that members may be reluctant to speak freely in a group meeting, distribute small index cards and ask people to write their questions and concerns on the card without identifying themselves. Then have the leader read the cards and, with the manager, respond to the items presented. Alternatively, ask members to prepare and submit their cards in advance of the meeting. This exercise will surface issues that, if they were to remain unspoken, could derail your team in the future.

- *Introductions of members.* Provide some time for members to introduce themselves to their teammates. Suggest that, at a minimum, the introductions include their skills, knowledge, and relevant experience as well as membership on other teams, both past and present. To humanize the exercise, ask that people talk about their hobbies, interests, family, and other outside activities. For a number of other options, go to tool #24, "Serious Fun at Team Meetings? You're Kidding!"

- *Draft of team charter.* It is helpful at the kick-off meeting to get started on the preparation of the team charter. The charter includes sections on mission, goals, objectives, time lines, responsibilities, and ground rules on meetings, decision making, communication, reports, and trust. At the kick-off meeting, begin the process by brainstorming ideas for inclusion in each of the sections. An effective approach is to divide the team into small task teams with each responsible for development of one or two sections. An action item from the meeting then becomes to complete the section for a report at the next team meeting.

## SAMPLE KICK-OFF MEETING NOTICE AND AGENDA

Name of Team, Board, or Group: ABC 101

Date of Meeting: December 3

Time: 9:25 A.M. to 11:37 A.M.

Venues: Milan Meeting Room: Como 202; U.S. Meeting Room: Madison 102

Dial-in Number: 877-555-1234

Pin Codes: Host: 5551234; Others: 10011

Key Meeting Outcomes: Key project objectives, understanding of management's expectations, clarification of initial issues associated with the team and the project, and drafting of team charter.

Pre-Meeting Preparation: Meet with your manager to discuss the project and your role on the team; prepare a list of questions and concerns you have about the project, the team, and your role.

## AGENDA

| Topic/Outcome | Time | Action | Person Responsible |
|---|---|---|---|
| 1. Introductions of team members | 15 min. | Meet your teammates | Timothy |
| 2. Presentation of initial project overview | 15 min. | Agreement on initial plan | Timothy |
| 3. Management's expectations of the project and team | 30 min. | Clarification of expectations | Jonathan |
| 4. Your concerns and questions | 30 min. | Responses to questions | Timothy & Jonathan |
| 5. Draft of team charter | 30 min. | Preliminary agreement on charter and task group assignments | All |
| 6. Agreement on next steps | 12 min. | List of steps and action items | All |

**Related Tools**

- Preparing for Your Next Meeting (tool #2)
- How to Prepare an Action Agenda (tool #3)
- Establishing Your Team's Ground Rules (tool #7)
- Serious Fun at Team Meetings? You're Kidding! (tool #24)

# 9

# PLANNING AN OFF-SITE MEETING THAT'S ON TARGET

## *Purpose*

Have you ever heard this comment: "Why don't we get away from the office for a few days and do some team building?" The next steps are pretty predicable: reserve space at the old reliable Rolling Hills Conference Center, hire that funny consultant who does those outdoor challenge games, and send out the meeting notice to everyone.

We're being a little cynical here, of course, but it's to make a point—an effective off-site team meeting requires more than just a tranquil setting and some team-building games. Specifically, a good off-site team meeting requires thoughtful planning built around a set of clear objectives.

An off-site meeting of a team, especially a global team, is a major financial investment. The costs associated with the meeting facility, travel expenses of the members, consulting services, and entertainment, as well as the opportunity costs associated with the members' time away from the job (that is, lost productivity) can be substantial. Therefore, the results also need to be substantial.

The purpose of this tool is to provide guidelines for a successful off-site team meeting.

### Tips for Planning an Effective Off-Site Team-Building Meeting

- *Be clear about the reasons for the meeting.* Why do you want to have this meeting? Make a list of the reasons. Where possible, involve team members, perhaps during a regular team meeting, in a brainstorming exercise designed to generate a list of reasons. This list should be your starting point.

- Is the team experiencing some problems?

- Have many new members joined the team?

- Is the project behind schedule?

- Is there conflict among some of the members?

- Is senior management dissatisfied with the way the team is working?

- Has the team not had a face-to-face meeting of all the members in more than a year?

- *Conduct a needs assessment.* The purpose of this data collection is to explore the reasons for the meeting in more depth to clarify and expand the list as well as add other reasons. Depending on your time and resources the data collection can be fast and simple or detailed and comprehensive. Here are some possibilities:

    - Conduct a discussion at a regular team meeting around a questions such as "What issues should we address at the off-site team building?"

    - Send out an anonymous team assessment survey to all team members to gather their perceptions of the team's effectiveness in various components of team success. An example of such a survey is the Drexler-Sibbet Team Performance Indicator, available at www.grove.com. Another such survey is the Parker Team Development Survey available from www.cpp.com.

    - Ask a consultant from Human Resources to interview team members with the goal of understanding their views of the issues, identifying effective and ineffective team practices as well ways the team can improve. Use these data as the basis for forming clear objectives for the meeting.

- *Prepare clear objectives for the meeting.* With the additional information from the needs assessment, you are now able to translate the list of reasons that were your starting point into a set a meeting outcomes. These objectives should identify the direction of the meeting and provide a clear focus by narrowing the scope to a manageable area of work. Don't concern yourself with making sure your objectives follow a standard format. As long as your goals specify an outcome, that is sufficient. For example:

- Prepare a plan to improve team relationships with our key stakeholders.

- Create a team charter, including a list of team norms.

- Members will get to know each other better.

- Develop three new viable product ideas.

- *Keep it practical and relevant.* It's OK to have fun along the way but be sure to maintain your focus on exercises and activities that move the team forward. Have a healthy balance between fun and games and practical outcomes that address the team issues that provide the rationale for the meeting in the first place. As a general rule, spend 60 percent to 75 percent of your time on practical team objectives with the remainder on light team activities. However, even the fun exercises should be relevant to the team's needs. For example, a team survival game can be fun and challenging but also teach members how to use the consensus method to make decisions.

- *Provide a structure (but not a rigid time schedule).* Your objectives provide a direction for the meeting outcomes but you should go with the flow of the group. In other words, if a topic or exercise really energizes the team and they want to explore it in depth, allow that to happen as long as the discussion remains relevant to the goal. Don't worry if you run out of time before all the identified issues are addressed. Sometimes it is just not possible to predict the interest level of team members in advance. At the end of the day or the end of the off-site meeting, if you have addressed some of the most important issues in depth and developed action plans for each, the off-site meeting should be seen as a success even if you didn't get to everything on the agenda.

- *Build in a follow-up process.* An off-site meeting should be seen less as an event and more as part of an ongoing process of team development. Therefore, be sure to build in time at the end of the off-site meeting to talk about

  - ◆ Accomplishments: What did we get done?

  - ◆ Next steps: What should we do next?

  - ◆ Follow-up: How will the plans will be implemented?

  - ◆ Assignments: Who will be responsible for various tasks?

  - ◆ Evaluation: Was the meeting successful?

In addition, include time at your next on-site team meeting to discuss the follow-up actions.

- *Select a site that supports your objective.* While we do not put this tip at the top of the list, the meeting environment can contribute to or detract from the goals of the off-site meeting. If one of the goals of the meeting is to have the members engage in some creative problem-solving about team issues, then holding your meeting in a dreary conference room in a dreary hotel will not help. And, if *off-site* is defined as a meeting in a room in another company building, then you may need to adjust your expectations. The mental and physical aspects of the environment are related. Comfortable, movable chairs, lots of light (preferably natural light), bright colors, healthy or fun food and drinks available at all times, whiteboards, flip charts, even small toys and tactile objects all contribute to creativity, risk taking, and relaxed problem solving. If a tight budget limits your ability to use an expensive conference center or hotel, here are some options:

  - ◆ Look for a nice room in a local library, university, or public building that is available at little or no cost.

- ◆ If you use a low-cost public room or a room in another company building, ask permission to decorate it to increase its appeal and alignment with your off-site meeting objectives.

- ◆ Adopt the "100-Mile Rule." This team ground rule states that members should act as if they are 100 miles away. In other words, they do not return to their office during breaks or at lunch time and colleagues cannot walk into the room during the meeting because they are "100 miles from home."

- *Turn off all electronic communication tools.* If you want focus and commitment, it is a good idea to adopt a ground rule that says all meeting participants will turn off their cell phones, beepers, BlackBerrys, computers (except to take notes or work on projects for the meeting itself, without sneaking peeks at incoming e-mail) when the meeting is in session. Explain that you will have several breaks during the course of the day when people can check and return messages. However, during the meeting people need to focus on the issues being discussed.

**Related Tools**

- Preparing for Your Next Meeting (tool #2)
- How to Prepare an Action Agenda (tool #3)
- Establishing Your Team's Ground Rules (tool #7)
- Serious Fun at Team Meetings? You're Kidding! (tool #24)

# 10

# YOUR OPENING ACT

## SETTING THE TONE FOR AN EXCELLENT TEAM MEETING

## *Purpose*

When it comes to meetings, the way you begin is an especially good predictor of how you will wind up. "Your Opening Act" is a list of tips for meeting facilitators who want to get meetings off to a great start. Customize these strategies as needed for your team.

### Tips for a Strong Start

- *Arrive or call in early.* Arriving early, calling in first, or getting online before the scheduled start of the meeting enables you to ensure that the technology is working properly. In turn, this means that the meeting will get off to a timely and smooth start. And, as the first person to arrive, you are in a position to greet the members each personally as they arrive, call in, or sign on.

- *Start on time.* The best way to embed the norm of "starting on time" is, of course, to start on time. Allow at most a five-minute lag, but then begin the meeting by saying, "We have a great deal to cover today, so let's begin on time." The more you make a practice of waiting for people, the more likely people will continue to arrive to meetings late. It is also important to respect the time of members who do arrive on time.

- *Welcome the members to the meeting.* "Good morning [or afternoon], all. How are you today?" For audio or video teleconference meetings, you may want to begin with something like this:

- "Can everyone hear [and see] all right?"
- "How are things in _____?"
- "The weather here is _____."
- "How's the weather in _____?"
- "Did you hear what happened in _____?"

And then, "We have a number of important issues to cover today, so let's get started."

- *Ask the members at each site to introduce themselves.* If this is a face-to-face meeting, introductions may not be necessary. However, if a new person joins the team, everyone (not just the new member) should be given an opportunity for personal introductions. If it is a teleconference, you may want to begin with:
  - "Let's see who is here today."
  - "Can we start with the people in Milan?"
  - "Who is on the phone and where are you?"
  - "And now let's have the folks from the Manchester introduce themselves?"

Generally, rather than have the leader call the roll, it is preferable to have the participants each speak up, giving their name and location as well as anything else they would like to add. To facilitate communication, you want to give members an opportunity to associate a name with a voice (and a face, for a videoconference) at the beginning of the meeting.

- *State the overall purpose of the meeting.* "The main purpose of today's meeting is to get an agreement on [specific issue] and make a decision about [some subset of that issue]. While we have some other issues to consider, this is the most important thing we need to accomplish by the end of today's meeting."

- *Review the agenda, especially the key outcomes for each item.* "Let's quickly go over the items on the agenda and clarify the outcome we seek for each one. On the first item, we need to make a final decision on whether to authorize an additional market study. The second issue requires that we consider approval of the amendment of the X product agreement. Finally, I know some of you have concerns about [another issue], and you will have a chance to air those concerns at the appropriate time."

- *Remind the members of the important ground rules, especially ones that may be relevant to today's meeting.* "I want to bring to your attention a couple of our more important meeting ground rules. Specifically, we agreed to use our laptops only to read materials related to today's meeting. In addition, given the length of the agenda today, it's very important that we all keep our comments both brief and on topic so as to ensure that we discuss all the issues on the agenda and finish on time."

- *Ask for feedback, including changes on the agenda.* "Finally, before we begin with item one, are there any changes to the agenda? Do we need to add any last-minute issues? Is there anything that should be deleted and handled off-line? Do we need to alter the order of the items for some reason?"

## Related Tools

- How to Prepare an Action Agenda (tool #3)
- Establishing Your Team's Ground Rules (tool #7)
- Staying on Track (tool #13)
- Communicating in a Videoconference (tool #16)
- Teleconference Tips (tool #17)

# 11

# E-MAIL EXCELLENCE

## *Purpose*

Nothing beats e-mail for speed, efficiency, and convenience. E-mail provides instant delivery, a built-in message thread, and a reliable record of important exchanges. But all this convenience has come at a price. E-mail is overused, and most workers feel tethered to their computers and handhelds just to keep pace with the volume.

This tool provides tips for using e-mail as the valuable, time-saving tool it's meant to be.

### Tips for Excellent E-Mail

- *To send or not to send?*

    - E-mail is one-way communication, so each message you send will generate one or more replies. Send fewer messages and you will also receive fewer. "Send to" and "cc" only those with a clear stake or interest in the message. Keep this in mind before selecting "Reply to All." *Does everyone on the list need to know you'll be attending the meeting?*

    - Pause before replying. Decide whether a response is truly necessary. *Will your note support the process or further the discussion?*

    - Resist the temptation to reply to each note right away. Doing so may cause you to create a reply when one isn't really needed. This practice also breaks up your day and can slow progress on critical tasks and deliverables. Scan your Inbox during the day and reply only to the notes that are truly urgent. Reserve time at the end of the day for the balance. *Does the sender need an immediate reply to make a decision or to progress on a specific initiative?*

♦ End the exchange as quickly as possible. When you reply, answer all questions in the original note directly, and anticipate and pre-empt follow-up questions by providing even more information. *What else is this person likely to need to move forward?*

- *E-mail or phone call?*

  ♦ Avoid using e-mail for urgent, controversial, or confidential messages. E-mail often lacks tone and doesn't convey emotion or the subtleties of conversation. When clarity and dialogue are important, or when a message must be kept private, call or meet in person. *Could this important message be misunderstood or get lost in the recipient's Inbox clutter?*

  ♦ Decide whether a call would save time. Quick confirmations, a simple yes or no, and other brief exchanges might be better suited to a phone call. *Is this an e-mail exchange or a conversation?*

  ♦ Pick up the phone every so often to make a personal connection with the people on your team. (And include your office and mobile phone numbers in your e-mail signature to make it easy to reach you by phone.) *Has it been more than two weeks since you actually spoke to this colleague?*

- *Break through the clutter.*

  ♦ Be descriptive and specific in your subject line. *Does the subject line provide enough information for recipients to decide whether to read the note right away or file it for later handling?*

  ♦ When you reply, check the subject line. Edit as needed to keep it up-to-date. *Is the subject line still clearly descriptive of the contents or has the topic changed during the exchange?*

- *Be brief, be brilliant, and be done!*

  ♦ Keep the note to a single screen. If your content is longer, write a brief e-mail and send the balance of the information as an attachment. *Is your e-mail longer than it needs to be? Can the same message be expressed in fewer words?*

◆ Since reading from a screen is more difficult than reading on paper, use bullets, numbers, paragraphs, and adequate spacing to make your note easier to read. *Is the note easy on the eyes?*

◆ Use complete sentences. Punctuate them. Use the spelling and grammar-checking functions, making sure that you understand the computer's advice and know that it is correct before you apply it. (Remember that the computer can't really read; it may propose alternate spellings that have nothing to do with your topic, and its grammar advice can be sadly misguided.) E-mail messages that are written with care are easier to read and minimize the number of exchanges. *Read from the recipient's perspective; is there any cause for confusion?*

◆ Avoid using idiomatic expressions that will elude people outside your country. *What words or phrases might be unfamiliar?*

## Related Tools

- Preparing for Your Next Meeting (tool #2)
- Achieving Clear Communication in a Multicultural Meeting (tool #18)
- After-Meeting Actions (tool #32)
- Managing External Communications (tool #33)

PART 2

# FACILITATING THE MEETING

# 12

# MEETING TIME MANAGEMENT

## *WHEN TO MEET, HOW LONG TO MEET, AND WHEN TO TAKE A BREAK*

## *Purpose*

Meeting facilitators are usually more concerned with managing the time *during* a meeting (see tool #13, "Staying on Track"). They try to ensure that a sufficient amount of time is devoted to each agenda item and that the meeting ends with all important issues addressed. Time management during a meeting is very important, but it is also important to consider the broader issues of meeting time management—the best day and time to meet, the length of the meeting, and, if a long meeting is required, the timing of breaks during the meeting.

The purpose of this tool is to provide guidance to meeting planners in these areas of meeting time management. While we recognize that some decisions about time management are dictated by circumstances such as time zone differences and the demands of deadlines, team leaders should use the options within their control to maximize their meeting time management.

### Tips for Deciding When to Meet

- Ask the members of your team when they prefer to meet. Check for such issues as competing meetings and time needed to get to the meeting room.

- Meet when the participants are best able to deal with the issues that need to be considered. Some days and times are better than others— as we suggest in the rest of the tips in this section.

- Avoid Monday mornings, when members may need to address issues that arose over the weekend. In addition, many people like to use Monday morning to finalize their plans for the coming week.

- Avoid Friday afternoons, when the energy level of meeting participants may be low. Friday afternoon is often a time used by members to complete assignments due by the end of the week. It is also a time that people like to use to prepare summaries or status reports and to plan their activities for the following week.

- Avoid the time right after lunch when body systems slow down and people tire. This means starting an afternoon meeting no earlier than 2:00 P.M.

- Avoid meeting very early in the morning, when many parents take their children to child care or school and getting to work may pose problems.

- A good time to meet is before lunch because it allows people to have lunch together after the meeting.

  - Working lunch meetings are usually undesirable because they eliminate the lunch break that gives people time to reflect and refresh and then be more effective for the rest of the day.

  - However, a team may elect to schedule a lunch meeting as a break from their usual routine. A new team may also decide to have lunch as part of their kick-off session. In these cases, if the meeting starts with the food (preferably light and healthy), this informal time can be used either as an opportunity to talk informally about the meeting topics or as an ice-breaker that gives members time to get to know each other.

- The best times to meet are between 9:30 A.M. and 12 noon and between 2:30 and 5:00 P.M.

- The best days to meet are Monday afternoon, Tuesday, Wednesday, Thursday, and Friday morning.

- Consider starting and ending your meeting at odd times. For example, your meeting may start at 10:12 A.M. and end at 11:47 A.M. This schedule serves two purposes: It gives members time to get to your meeting from an earlier meeting that ended on the hour, and it gets everyone's attention and may increase the likelihood of on-time arrival.

## Tips for Determining How Long to Meet

- Aim for fairly short sessions if at all possible. After about two hours, meeting effectiveness drops very dramatically.

- A meeting should go no longer than 90 minutes without a break.

- Of course, many project team meetings must run longer than one or two hours because of the difficulty of getting all the members together. In that case, breaks must be built into the agenda.

## Tips for Scheduling a Break

- Try to schedule a break every hour.

- It is better to schedule two 10-minute breaks rather than one 15- or 20-minute break.

- Breaks should not be too long (more than 20 minutes), or members are likely to lose focus or get involved in other tasks.

- Breaks should not be too short (5 minutes); it's best to give members ample time to refresh and refocus on the agenda. In setting the break time, consider the toilet facilities available for men and for women, bearing in mind that women need more time than men to make use of them.

- One fun and effective exception is the one-minute "stretch" break, where members stand and exercise their arms and legs by simply extending them out and back.

- Another ground rule used by some teams allows any member to call a short break whenever the group energy feels low, it looks like people need a bio-break, or the meeting has gone on for too long.

- A two and one-half to three-hour project team meeting should include at least two breaks. If time is limited, consider one 10-minute break and one stretch break.

- An important factor is managing the break time in such a way that members hold to the time allocated for the break and return to the meeting on time. Since the time on each person's watch may differ, do not ask them to return at a specific time (for example, 10:30 A.M.). The best approach is to ask members to return to the meeting 10 minutes from the current time on their watch or the clock in the meeting room. If necessary, walk into the hallway and ask members to return to the meeting.

### Related Tools

- Preparing for Your Next Meeting (tool #2)
- Defining Team Meeting Roles (tool #4)
- Components of a New Team Kick-Off Meeting (tool #8)
- Staying on Track (tool #13)
- How to Get Effective Participation (tool #14)
- Serious Fun at Team Meetings? You're Kidding! (tool #24)
- Eating Well = Meeting Well (tool #25)
- Ending Meetings On Time and On Target (tool #26)

# 13

# STAYING ON TRACK

## *Purpose*

One of the most frustrating and often confounding problems that derails meeting effectiveness is a discussion that slowly migrates from the agenda topic. It is frustrating for team members because they feel their time is being wasted. And it is confounding for the meeting facilitator because correcting the problem may require directly addressing the behavior.

It is important to note that it is the *behavior*—and, more important, the impact of the behavior—that must be confronted, not the character or motivation of the members involved in the digression.

We see three main factors that lead meetings off track: topic migration, topic magnification, and time mismanagement. With migration—sometimes referred to as "being in the weeds"—an irrelevant topic (for example, getting project partners to deliver on their commitments) or intellectually challenging (for example, the intricacies of a study design) may be more interesting to everyone at the table than the agenda item under discussion. With magnification, what happens is that an agenda item is of great interest to a few members of the team, who are highly engaged and interested and can discuss it endlessly. At the same time, the rest of the members have little or no interest in the subject. As a result, they disengage, becoming mere observers or worse, falling into dysfunctional behavior such as doing other work or having side conversations.

The two biggest time mismanagement problems that compromise meeting excellence are starting the meeting late and not honoring the time allocations for the agenda items. Don't be concerned about occasional lapses. For example, there is no need to worry if on occasion your meeting starts 5 minutes late or every so often you spend an extra 15 minutes on a topic and then shave some time off subsequent (and with reasonable forethought) less important topics. The issue here is a pattern—an embedded norm—of mismanagement.

This tool provides strategies for getting your meeting back on track.

## Tips for Controlling Topic Migration

- *Intervene with a casual but clear comment.* "It looks like we have drifted a bit. Let's come back and focus on . . ."

- *Address the diversion directly.* "We are now discussing [irrelevant material], and while the topic may be interesting, it is taking us away from the important issue of [agenda stuff] that we must decide today."

- *Pointing out the impact of the drift.* "We have just spent ten minutes focusing on [one nontopic], which has cut into the time allocated on the agenda to develop a plan to [do something essential]."

## Tips for Limiting Topic Magnification

- *Postpone the discussion.* Ask the small group to meet outside the team meeting and, if necessary, report back at the next meeting.

- *Postpone the rest of the meeting.* If the small group agrees to complete their discussion in 10 to 15 minutes, suggest that they continue now while the rest of the team takes a break.

- *Refer the issue to the meeting's "parking lot."* This is the segment at the end of the agenda where a team can place important issues raised during a meeting without being on the planned agenda. At the end of the meeting, all items in the parking lot are reviewed for inclusion on the agenda of the next meeting, assignment to a subteam for study, or assignment to a member as an action item. See the discussion of the "parking lot attendant" in tool #4, "Defining Team Meeting Roles."

- *Avoid the problem up front.* When you prepare your meeting agenda, try to minimize the number of topics that don't need the whole team's attention. Encourage people to use subgroup gatherings for issues that concern only a small segment of the team.

**Tips for Preventing Time Mismanagement**

- *Avoid starting late.* As the meeting facilitator, a key part of your role is to arrive early, be sure the technology is up and running and the room setup is acceptable, arrange your papers, and get focused and ready to begin on time. The best way to get back on the time track is to *simply start on time* with whoever is in the room or online at the scheduled start time.

  - *Provide due warning.* If your meetings have consistently started late in the past, you might announce at the end of a meeting that you intend to start the next meeting on time (and reinforce this with a similar statement in the meeting notice). Starting on time also demonstrates respect for the members who do arrive on time.

  - *Establish a new norm.* As an alternative, at the end of a meeting, mention the consistent late start and ask for members' thoughts on the reasons for the late starts as well as suggestions for starting future meetings on time.

- *Try to stick to the estimated time allocated for agenda items.* When you take more time to complete the first few agenda items, you naturally have less time to consider the final few items. If every agenda follows a similar sequence of items, the same topics and people will be adversely affected at every meeting. The net result can be demoralizing for those people, as it appears to diminish their importance to the team.

- *Set up for success before the meeting.* When you develop the agenda, ask the member responsible for the agenda item for a *realistic* estimate of the time needed to consider the issue.

- *Keep an eye on both the clock and the agenda during the meeting.* As you approach the end of the time allocated for the item, ask the person responsible for the item if it will be possible to finish in the next five minutes. If not, ask how much longer it will take.

◆ If more time is needed, ask team members if they would like to continue now (with the understanding that the meeting will either go beyond the scheduled end time or other agenda items will be reduced in time or deleted), add the topic to the agenda for the next meeting, or ask a subgroup to consider the issue and report at the next meeting.

◆ If you know that most of the members will want to comment on an issue, consider instituting a temporary ground rule that limits comments to a specific amount of time (for example, two minutes). Another ground rule used by some teams states that before a person can speak again on a issue, all other members who want to comment have a chance to speak at least once.

◆ If the matter has migrated too far, refer it to the meeting's parking lot.

Finally, remember that keeping the meeting focused is every team member's responsibility! Establish this idea as one of your team norms.

**Related Tools**

- How to Prepare an Action Agenda (tool #3)
- Defining Team Meeting Roles (tool #4)
- Establishing Your Team's Ground Rules (tool #7)
- Meeting Time Management (tool #12)
- How to Get Effective Participation (tool #14)

# 14

# HOW TO GET EFFECTIVE PARTICIPATION

## *Purpose*

If the key outcome of your meeting is to make a decision, solve a problem, develop a plan, or anything else that requires the expertise of team members, you need to make use of effective participation tools. Since the information, knowledge, and experience needed to answer the questions resides in the group, your task as the meeting facilitator is to bring it all to the table and then focus it on the desired result.

Your sometimes difficult challenge is to get the necessary participation while managing the time available and staying focused on the goal. For related tips, see tool #13, "Staying on Track."

The purpose of this tool is to provide meeting leaders with a repertoire of participation techniques for obtaining, maintaining, and channeling the discussion to the end result. The specific focus here is on the variety of questions that can be used by a facilitator to accomplish many different participation goals, including asking the right kind of question to get the information or other response most useful in a given situation. We also include tips for dealing with the special situation of getting participation from a quiet member.

### Types of Questions

- *Open-ended question.* This is the staple of the successful facilitator. It is a question that gives people a great deal of latitude in their response because it cannot be answered with either a yes or a no. It is the best questioning technique for getting participation. Therefore, the skill of asking effective open-ended questions must be mastered. Most good open-ended questions begin with What, How, or Why. For example:

    ◆ What is the impact of this change on the project plan?

- How will this cut in the budget affect our schedule?

- Why are we having problems recruiting people for this study?

- *Closed-ended question.* This question type is used when you want a direct and specific answer. It is a question that requires a yes or a no or other brief response. A closed-ended question can be coupled with a follow-up probe to obtain more information. Some examples:

  - Has the application been filed with the zoning authority?

  - How many participants do we have registered?

  - Are we going to open a new site?

- *Overhead question.* This is a question asked to the whole group. It allows any member of the team to respond. It can be either an open-ended or closed-ended question, although we recommend greater use of the open-ended variety.

  - How do you feel about the new guidelines?

  - What are some ways we can deal with this issue?

  - What is your experience in working with this group?

  - Has anyone who's dealt with this problem in the past got some insight to offer?

- *Direct question.* Used sparingly and carefully, directing a question to a specific person can be effective. The general guideline is that you may call on someone if you are asking a question that falls within their area of expertise or you see a nonverbal cue (for example, looking alert and eager, leaning forward) that indicates they want to participate.

  - Karla, is this consistent with our marketing plan?

  - Raja, how do you feel about this proposed change?

  - Clarisse, you look like you have something to say about this issue . . .

- *Re-direct question.* As a facilitator, you have the goal of optimizing communication among team members and minimizing direct question-and-answer dialogues between you and specific members. The re-direct question is one way to address this goal. The technique here is to catch a question from a member directed to you and re-direct it to another member. Here's how it works in practice:

- ◆ Mario, that's an interesting question. Kim, how do you feel about it?

- ◆ Pierre is asking an important question about the marketing strategy. Andrew, from the Marketing Department's perspective, how would it work out?

- ◆ Diane, can you shed any light on the issues raised in Mark's question?

- *Relay question.* Similar in approach to the re-direct, the relay question takes a member's question directed to the leader and sends it back to the whole group as an overhead question. The goal is to both minimize the focus on you and increase member participation, as in the following examples:

  - ◆ Anne makes an interesting point. How do the rest of you feel about it?

  - ◆ Rachel, that's an important question. Let's see what other people think we should do about it . . .

  - ◆ Jacquin has asked me to make a decision on this issue but many of you have much more experience in this area. What do you think we should do about the problem?

- *Probe question.* A question that asks for more information is typically a follow-up to another question such as an open-ended question. With the probe you are looking for greater depth, more breadth, some examples, and a rationale. Here are some examples:

  - • What else can you tell us about the problems with this contractor?

- ◆ What are some examples of how this will work in our situation?

- ◆ You seem to indicate that the customers are very unhappy with the results. What were some of their specific complaints?

- *Summary or consensus-seeking question.* As you come to the end of a discussion or seem to be nearing a decision, you can use a question to help the group get to the desired outcome or move the meeting along to the next topic. A summary-seeking question may be asked directly to a specific person or as an overhead to the group, as in the following samples:

  - ◆ Michele, am I hearing correctly that you want to see us adopt this new procedure on a trial basis?

  - ◆ It appears to me as if we have an agreement to enter into negotiations with Market Quest. Is that correct?

  - ◆ Since everyone has addressed the issue and we don't seem to have any objections, am I correct in saying that we have reached a consensus to stop this trial run at the end of the month?

- *Paraphrase question.* One of the most powerful tools in the facilitator's kit is the ability to restate what a person has said in such a way as to capture the meaning and often the intent of the statement. A corollary skill is to use it judiciously. Paraphrasing should be used when a statement is critical to the outcome of the discussion, may be confusing to others, or expresses a feeling that may represent a widespread sentiment in the group. Overuse of paraphrasing can become annoying and a drain on team progress. Here are some examples:

  - ◆ What I hear you saying is you want us to change the frequency of this service. Is that correct?

  - ◆ Are you asking us to change the frequency to reflect these early results from the customer satisfaction survey?

  - ◆ Before we move to the next item, let me be sure I understand you correctly. It sounds like you want us to allocate funds to begin a new study to test this idea. Is that what I am hearing?

- *Consequences question.* Sometimes referred to as a what-if scenario, this type of question asks team members to consider the consequences of their suggestion, solution, or decision. As a facilitator you want meeting participants to look beyond the immediate situation and into the future. Ultimately, your questions push members to think about the costs and benefits of their actions, as in the following samples:

  - What will be the impact of this decision on sales in Latin America?

  - Gerald, what do you believe will be the company's overall market share in this area?

  - It looks like we are saying we need to seek out another contractor for this task. What are the political consequences of that decision?

## Tips for Getting Participation from a Quiet Member

- *Look for nonverbal cues that the person wants to make a contribution.* When you see someone lean forward, seem to have a quizzical expression, or move their head in agreement or disagreement, you may ask something like, "Gwen, it looks like you have something to say about this topic; I would love to hear your thoughts about it."

- *When the person does offer an opinion or provide some information, react positively.* Respond with something like, "Thanks, Gwen, for that thoughtful response. Let's consider Gwen's idea and see where it takes us."

- *Ask an easy question that provides an opportunity to share knowledge or demonstrate experience:* "Sean, I know you have a great deal of experience in Asia/Pacific marketing. Can you tell how we should approach that area with this new service?"

- *Look the person into participation.* When a question has been asked by you or another team member, look directly at the normally silent person with your face in a friendly expression that indicates you are interested in hearing their response.

- *Give the person an action item that requires them to report at a future meeting.* After the meeting, ask if you can help with the report.

- *Speak with the person privately.* Express your appreciation of their expertise and desire that they be a significant contributor to the work of the team. Ask if there is anything you can do to facilitate their participation.

## Keys to Asking a Good Question

- *Be brief and the point.* Ask the question, then be quiet and wait for a response. Avoid long introductions and detailed explanatory statements.

- *Make it a real question*—not a statement hidden in question form, especially if the alleged question contains your recommended answer. For example, avoid saying things like, "Don't you think that we should ask the steering committee to support this change?"

- *Use clear language that is easily understood by all members of the team.* Avoid arcane technical terms, esoteric scientific references, and slang that is only understood by certain cultural groups.

- *Do not ask a question that is designed to find fault.* You job is to bring out information that will help the team reach the desired outcome, not prove someone wrong. Stop yourself when you even think about asking a question that is something like, "Hans, isn't it true that the product design was faulty from the very beginning?"

## Final Thoughts on Getting Effective Participation

- *Prime the pump.* When people do contribute ideas, be encouraging ("tell us more") and supportive ("thanks for your input").

- *Remember that people can be participating even though they are silent.* They may be listening and considering the facts and opinions. If you see nonverbal cues of ongoing participation (nods, taking occasional notes, sitting back but watching each speaker attentively), it may not be necessary or even desirable to try to get someone to speak.

- *Sometimes your best facilitation strategy is to just be quiet.* If you see good interaction among a variety of members, you have no need to say anything. Just let the conversation continue as long it is moving toward some positive action.

- *Withhold your opinion as long as possible.* The best approach is to encourage and allow team members to express their points of view before you share your expertise or data.

- *Be aware of your participation.* The facilitator should rarely be the dominant participant in a discussion. If you find yourself dominating the discussion, back off and try to get others involved.

## Related Tools

- Meeting Time Management (tool #12)
- Staying on Track (tool #13)
- Building a Foundation of Trust (tool #15)
- Communicating in a Videoconference (tool #16)
- Teleconference Tips (tool #17)
- How to Make a Decision (tool #19)
- Responding to Nonverbal Communication (tool #22)

## 15

# BUILDING A FOUNDATION OF TRUST

## *Purpose*

In the practical world of team meetings, trust is the most elusive of all ideas. And yet trust may be the most important of all meeting elements to achieve. It may also be the most difficult to attain.

Trust is at the foundation of effective meetings and successful teamwork. When there is a high level of trust:

- Members expect action items to be completed on time.

- The team leader devotes minimal time and effort to checking up and following up with members between meetings.

- Members feel free to express any and all opinions at meetings.

- Misunderstandings and other types of miscommunication are rare.

- Members show a high level of respect for the expertise and opinions expressed at meetings.

- Key stakeholders rely on the team's commitments without reservations.

The purpose of this tool is to suggest actions by the team facilitator and team members that will help your team establish and maintain a foundation of trust in team meetings.

We strongly recommend that your team consider formally adopting some of these behaviors. See tool #7, "Establishing Your Team's Ground Rules."

**Trust-Building Tips for the Team Facilitator**

- Promise only what you honestly expect to deliver.

- Keep your promises and commitments.

- Empower members to make decisions and act on behalf of the team.

- Be open and listen to the opinions of team members.

- Communicate with members openly and honestly, without distorting any information.

- Assume members will complete action items without checking up on them; follow up only to offer help.

- Provide members with appropriate credit and recognition for their accomplishments.

- Admit your own mistakes, errors in judgment, and inability to meet commitments.

- Provide stakeholders with honest assessments of project status—successes as well as actual and potential problems.

- When members experience problems, offer to help rather than trying to fix blame.

**Trust-Building Tips for Team Members**

- Accept action items, due dates, and other team commitments only when you have a high level of confidence in your ability to deliver.

- Maintain the confidentiality of information told to you privately.

- Even when you disagree with them, treat the opinions of teammates with respect.

- Admit your own mistakes, errors in judgment, and inability to meet commitments.

- Communicate honestly with teammates without distorting information.

- Do not take sole credit for work done in collaboration with others.

- Demonstrate confidence in your teammates' ability to deliver high-quality work.

- Ensure that your actions, including nonverbal behaviors, are consistent with your words. See tool #22, "Responding to Nonverbal Communication."

- Be willing to work outside your defined job responsibilities to support a teammate or help the team accomplish a goal.

- Do not send mixed messages that keep teammates from knowing where you stand. (For example, don't say you are willing to help out at any time but then be unavailable or "very busy" when a specific request is sent to you.)

### Related Tools

- Establishing Your Team's Ground Rules (tool #7)
- How to Get Effective Participation (tool #14)
- How to Make a Decision (tool #19)
- Resolving Conflicts in a Team Meeting (tool #21)
- Responding to Nonverbal Communication (tool #22)
- Managing Meeting Monsters (tool #23)

# 16

# COMMUNICATING IN A VIDEOCONFERENCE

## *Purpose*

A videoconference is a wonderful tool for conducting a team meeting when members are located in several sites. It is helpful to be able to see as well as hear all the members of the team at various company locations. However, the technology presents some communications challenges that are not present in a face-to-face meeting.

The purpose of this tool is to provide tips for both the meeting facilitator and team members, designed to increase the effectiveness of communication in a videoconference.

### Tips for the Meeting Facilitator

- Arrive early to ensure the equipment is turned on and up and running effectively.

- Greet people as they arrive at the rooms at the various sites.

- Since most videoconference systems include a two- or three-second transmission delay, effective active listening can be difficult and people at multiple sites often wind up speaking at the same time. To accommodate this "technical difficulty," you may need to remind the participants to allow a few seconds after the person finishes before they respond. And, of course, as in a face-to-face meeting, they should not interrupt the speaker in the middle of a thought.

- When introducing a new agenda item or asking a question, be a model of effective videoconference behavior by being brief and getting to the point quickly.

- Tactfully intervene when a member makes a lengthy comment or long introduction to a new topic. ("Greg, let me see if I can summarize your point so we can move on to hear how other people feel about it . . .")

- Since a videoconference requires more visual and auditory concentration than a face-to-face meeting, consider a brief break at least every 60 to 90 minutes. Sometimes just a quick stretch break in the room is all that a group requires.

- Take advantage of the video component to notice nonverbal communication, especially body language or facial expressions that indicate strong reactions of either agreement or disagreement. For example, if you notice members rolling their eyes or shaking their heads after a comment, you may want to say something like, "Hans, it looks like you disagree with the direction we're going. What is your opinion on the subject?" It is always best to respond to nonverbal cues with a question rather than a statement such as "Hans, you obviously don't agree with the proposal" since nonverbal communication can be difficult to read—no matter how obvious it looks to you, it may not be real, and the camera complicates the problem.

- Use the video to take note of signs of boredom, fatigue, or other indications of lack of involvement. When you see these signs, consider a brief break to refresh and reenergize the group.

## Tips for the Meeting Participant

- Remember that the microphone pod is very sensitive to sound; therefore, speak in your normal voice without shouting or leaning into the mike.

- Avoid side conversations; the mike will pick them up and the cross-talk will make it difficult to hear the person speaking. At times, a side conversation at one site becomes the center of attention at another site.

- Do not shuffle papers near the mike since it will interfere with audio transmission.

- When someone is presenting at another site, you may want to use the mute button at your site to prevent the transmission of background noise.

- When asking a question, be brief, get to the point quickly, then pause and wait for a response. Avoid long-winded prefaces and extensive background introductions to your questions.

- Avoid wearing small, busy patterns because they make it more difficult for the camera to focus. Solid, vibrant, or pastel colors send a clearer picture. Also avoid ornate or flashy jewelry that may reflect light and distort the video image.

- Try to avoid unpleasant hand or facial gestures or eating during a meeting. Remember that the people at other sites are looking at you just as you're looking at them—you're all on television for each other.

- Try not to move around a lot during a videoconference. Your image can appear distorted to the people in the other site until you stop moving.

**Related Tools**

- Preparing for Your Next Meeting (tool #2)
- Your Opening Act (tool #10)
- Staying on Track (tool #13)
- How to Get Effective Participation (tool #14)
- Building a Foundation of Trust (tool #15)
- Teleconference Tips (tool #17)
- Achieving Clear Communication in a Multicultural Meeting (tool #18)

- Presenting at a Team Meeting (tool #20)
- Responding to Nonverbal Communication (tool #22)
- Managing Meeting Monsters (tool #23)

# 17

# TELECONFERENCE TIPS

## *Purpose*

The most common electronic communications tool used by global teams is the teleconference. It takes the lead because it is easy to set up, rarely breaks down, and is relatively inexpensive. The typical teleconference meeting has a group of people in a conference room at one location, sometimes a second group at another location, and individual members at various other locations around the world. For the groups, a large speakerphone allows members around the conference table to hear the contributions of people from other locations. Individual members use their handset or cell phone.

While many of the guidelines for effective videoconferencing apply as well to the audio-only teleconference, many distinct techniques contribute to a successful teleconference. See tool #16, "Communicating in a Videoconference."

### Tips for Meeting Facilitators

- Before the meeting, send each participant a copy of the agenda and the required reading material and slides.

- Arrive early and call in to make sure the teleconference support is operating. Arriving early also allows you to greet everyone individually as they call in.

- Begin by asking the participants to take turns identifying themselves and their locations.

- If time permits, ask the participants to say something (for example, about the weather) that will help identify their voices to the other members.

- Refer to the agenda, state the key outcome of the meeting, and review the agenda items.

- If necessary, review the key norms, especially the one about no multi-tasking (doing other work during the meeting).

- At the beginning of the meeting, ask members to identify themselves before they speak and, if necessary, to specify to whom their remarks are directed.

- If you know any of the participants have insights or questions about the issue but have not spoken, call their names and ask if they have opinions to offer. ("Kim, you know a great deal about concurrent engineering, what can you tell us about this problem?")

- Since it is easy during a teleconference for members to talk over one another, enforce the norm of one person speaking at a time. Stop people if they start to speak before someone else is done.

- Summarize all action items and decisions as they occur during the meeting.

- When conflicts (such as professional differences of opinion) arise during a teleconference, carefully state or ask the members to state both sides of the issue before trying to work toward a solution. Recognize that it is more difficult to resolve conflicts during a teleconference than face-to-face. Resolution may require some off-line discussion.

- At the end of the meeting, summarize the key decisions and action items and, when time permits, ask members to evaluate the meeting.

**Tips for Team Members**

- If a subgroup of the team is meeting in a conference room at your location, join the group in that room. Do not call in from your office unless some emergency or very high-priority issue requires that you remain there.

- Try not to call in on a cell phone because of the unreliability of the service in some locations.

- If you must use a cell phone, do not call from a car that you are driving. Instead, get to a location where the cellular service is good—one with no dead zones and background noise. It is very distracting, for example, to hear traffic noise on the line during a meeting. The best location is a place where you can sit and take notes. In addition, in some locations (for example, New Jersey) it is illegal to use a cell phone while driving without a hands-free device. Most important, it can be dangerous.

- Speak up and look toward the speakerphone or into the handset or cell phone.

- Let speakers finish their thoughts before you begin your contribution. If you are unsure, ask, "Lars, are you finished? I have something to add on that point."

- Since you can't see nonverbal cues, the tone of some comments may be easy to misinterpret. If you are unsure about the intention of the previous comment, use your active listening skills. ("Jonathan, as I understand it, you are saying that we do not have enough data to support that conclusion.")

- If your comments or presentation are based on a document sent out in advance of the meeting, remind the other members that they may wish to access the document and follow along as you speak.

- Do not multi-task (do other work) during the meeting. It is considered by other members to be rude and disrespectful.

- Put your phone on mute if the background noise in your location is loud.

- If you must leave before the meeting is over, tell the meeting facilitator before or at the beginning of the meeting. When you depart, sign off by saying good-bye to your teammates. Do not just leave or hang up.

**Related Tools**

- Staying on Track (tool #13)
- How to Get Effective Participation (tool #14)
- Building a Foundation of Trust (tool #15)
- Communicating in a Videoconference (tool #16)
- Managing Meeting Monsters (tool #23)

# 18

# ACHIEVING CLEAR COMMUNICATION IN A MULTICULTURAL MEETING

## *Purpose*

Breakdowns in communication in meetings happen for many reasons. However, the purpose of this tool is to focus on the cultural aspects of language that inhibit clear communication. More specifically, the focus is on the English language, since it is the language used in most company meetings. Americans speak a variation of the language that sometimes can be difficult for people from other countries to comprehend, even people with great proficiency in English. While the focus of this tool is on language, it is important to note that nonverbal cues (such as eye contact or touching) often mean different things in different cultures and may also be a barrier to clear communication.

Clear communication in a multicultural meeting will lead to a variety of positive results:

- Participatory consensus decisions
- Clear communication of facts and opinion
- Effective use of team resources
- Practical conflict resolution
- More efficient time management
- Higher levels of trust among teammates
- Increased morale

*Note:* This tool draws heavily on a paper by Ira Asherman, "Language, Culture and the Drug Development Process," *DIA Today,* 2005, *5*(3), 28.

In meetings, ineffective communication results in many negative outcomes:

- Waste of time and resources
- Poor decisions
- Missed opportunities
- Useless conflict

In this tool you will find recommendations aimed at Americans since English is their primary (and often only) language, ideas for people from other cultures, and tips for meeting facilitators who play a critical role in ensuring clear communication.

### Suggestions for Americans Whose Primary Language Is English

- *Speak slowly and enunciate.* Many Americans speak too quickly to be easily understood by people whose primary language is not English.

- *Avoid long, complicated statements.* Get to the point directly and state it clearly. Minimize long and convoluted prefaces.

- *Avoid colloquial expressions* such as "heard it through the grapevine," "cut to the chase," "tackle the issues head on," and "beating around the bush." People unfamiliar with the expressions will translate the words just as they are spoken, picking up a different meaning than you intended (if they pick up anything at all).

- *Minimize sports analogies and slang,* especially those from uniquely American sports such as baseball that have no meaning in Europe. It is confusing to most non-Americans to hear that something is "way off base," or "not in the ballpark." Despite the fact that basketball is played in Europe, most non-Americans will not understand when you refer to something as a "slam dunk."

- *Do not tell jokes.* Jokes rarely translate well since the premise is often culture and language specific. If you have to explain a joke, the humor is lost. On the other hand, it is not necessary to eliminate all fun from meetings. A humorous remark about a project or situation that is easily understood by all team members can contribute to a relaxed, informal atmosphere.

- *Practice good active listening skills:*

  - Allow other people to finish their thoughts before you respond.

  - Pause and give other members some time to process what has been said and formulate a response.

  - Paraphrase what the other person has said before you respond.

  - Ask questions or ask for clarification if you do not understand or disagree with what has been said.

- *Use multichannel communications.* You increase the possibility that your intended message will be accurately received if you support your verbal comments with a written document that presents the same information. For example, a list of bullet points on the screen or in a handout provides other members with an alternative method of receiving the same information you present verbally. And, of course, it is helpful to send the presentation or document out to all members in advance of the meeting so it can reviewed quietly and carefully. (This does not mean you should read your bullet points. See tool #20, "Presenting at a Team Meeting," for more information.)

- *Learn as much as you can about communication patterns of other cultures.* For example, in some cultures in Latin America and the Far East, it is not acceptable to disagree with someone holding a higher rank in the organization. On the other hand, assuming individuals will act in a certain manner simply because they are from a specific country is a mistake. The best advice: get to know your specific teammates and develop sensitivity to how they communicate.

### Suggestions for Non-Primary English Speakers

- *Ask questions if you do not understand what has been said.* If another person uses a word, phrase, or some form of jargon or slang that you do not understand, ask for clarification. Also ask if you believe you disagree with what you're hearing.

- *Remember that being assertive about your communication needs is important, no matter how difficult it can sometimes be.* For many people, silence means understanding and agreement. In other words, your U.S. teammates may assume that if you say nothing, you both understand and agree with what is being said.

- *Use your active listening skills to ensure that you understand what has been said.* You might say something like, "Erika, if I understood you correctly, you are proposing that we change the release date for XK7." In meetings where asking questions or seeking clarification is difficult, speak to a teammate or the team leader at a break or after the meeting.

- *Before the meeting, review all the documents sent in advance and note items that are not clear or complete.* Seek clarification from colleagues in your area about words or phrases that are not clear. Formulate your questions for the meeting. It is also helpful to let the meeting leader or facilitator know before the meeting that you have questions or require clarification about a particular agenda item or document. The leader can then ensure that you are included in the discussion.

### Suggestions for Meeting Facilitators

- *Stop members when they use a colloquial expression, unusual jargon, or slang.* Ask for an explanation—despite the advice to members to speak up, you cannot assume that everyone will do so.

- *Periodically summarize key agreements and action items.* This will help make sure that everyone understands and agrees with what has been decided.

- *Interrupt members who are making a long statement and paraphrase the key portion of the statement.* This will make it easier for other members to understand their point.

- *Don't simply ask, "Do you understand?"* People rarely like to admit they do not understand; it implies they are incompetent. Instead, paraphrase what has been said with words that are more easily understood.

- *Observe members of the group for nonverbal signs of lack of understanding* (such as frowns or furrowed brows). If you sense that some key points are being missed, ask the speaker to review the items or summarize the points yourself. In addition, you can stop the discussion or presentation at key points and facilitate a discussion using some open-ended questions like these:

  - "Hans has covered a number of important issues. What questions or comments do you have on what he has said so far?"

  - "Let's stop at this point and review the key points of our plan. Now, how do the rest of you feel about what is being proposed?"

  - "There is a good deal of new and complex information in this report. Before we move forward, what items require further clarification?"

- *Observe members of the group for nonverbal signs that someone has something to contribute* but is taking some time to formulate thoughts on the matter (for example, leaning forward, or leaning back and looking up). It may require that you slow down a member who speaks quickly and then wants to get right into a discussion or reach a decision. You can say something like "Jonathan, we have heard a great deal from you today on this topic. Let's hear from some other people." Then, intervene with something like, "Barbara, it looks like you would like to comment on this point."

- *Set aside some time at a team meeting for a discussion of ways to improve cross-cultural communication* if you suspect that the issue is interfering with the work of the team as a whole. The outcome of the session should be some norms or guidelines for team communication.

**Related Tools**

- How to Get Effective Participation (tool #14)
- Building a Foundation of Trust (tool #15)
- How to Make a Decision (tool #19)
- Presenting at a Team Meeting (tool #20)
- Resolving Conflicts in a Team Meeting (tool #21)

# 19

# HOW TO MAKE A DECISION

## *Purpose*

The business of teams is decision making. In many ways, it is the reason most teams exist. Teams make decisions to spend money and to cut spending. They make decisions to approve new projects and to eliminate existing projects. Teams approve plans and documents and decide to alter or do away with them completely. Teams decide all sorts of things, and most of the deciding takes place in meetings.

A team meeting is usually the best place to make an effective decision. *And what does an effective decision look like?* Here are some critical factors:

- All members have an opportunity to participate in the process.
- Everyone agrees to and understands how the decision will be made.
- Many sides of the issue are considered.
- Members are open to opposing points of view.
- The decision is consistent with the team's goals and aligned with the organization's goals and strategy.
- All members support the decision and willingly help to implement it.

The purpose of this tool is to

- Help teams and team facilitators determine how to make a decision by providing a description of various decision-making methods, including their advantages and disadvantages.

- Help teams and team facilitators choose a decision method that is most appropriate for the situation in which they find themselves.

- Provide team facilitators with insight into the consensus decision-making method, including the following points:

  - What it is.
  - When to use it.
  - When not to use it.
  - The conditions associated with an effective consensus.
  - How to reach an effective consensus.

## Decision-Making Methods in Team Meetings

1. *Autocratic.* In this approach, the team leader makes the decision with no input from any of the members. Repellent as it may sound when stated so baldly, for many decisions, this style is both appropriate and effective:

   - When there is no value to be gained to obtaining input from members because they have no experience in this area.

   - When a quick decision is necessary (as in an emergency) or required (by senior management or a government agency).

   - When only one solution is correct, such as a decision required by law or company policy.

   - When team members have empowered the leader to make all such decisions.

   - When the members are aware that the leader is making the decision and understand the rationale for making the decision in this manner.

   *Potential Problems*
   - The decision may not be based on the best available information.

- Members may be less likely to support the execution of the decision.

- The decision may actually decrease team members' sense of the importance of their role.

- It may undermine team effectiveness if members are not aware of the conditions that made an independent decision necessary, believe they should have provided some input into the decision, or are not informed of the decision by the leader.

*Facilitator Comments*

- "I wanted to inform you that I submitted the corporate budget form to the Finance Office yesterday in order to meet their deadline."

- "At the business unit meeting last week I told the group that the ABXY customer service center will begin in the third quarter of next year."

2. *Participative.* The leader asks for the opinions of members and incorporates their views in the decision-making process. However, final authority for making the decision remains with the leader. This approach is both popular and useful in many team situations:

   - When the members have experience and insight into the issue to be decided.

   - When the leader lacks experience and knowledge of the topic and values the input of members.

   - When members need to feel they are part of the process.

   - When the leader is truly open to considering different points of view and incorporating these ideas in the decision-making process.

   - When the leader wants to increase the likelihood of members' supporting the implementation of the decision.

- When organizational policies or established norms require that the leader retain final responsibility for the decision.

*Potential Problems*

- Members may feel their input is not really valued, especially if the leader does not seem to be listening.

- If the manager does not use the input, members may lose interest in providing their ideas in the future.

*Facilitator Comments*

- "We have been asked for our opinion on the potential revenue loss of delaying the introduction of ABXY until the third quarter, and I would like to your input on this."

- "Although I am ultimately accountable for this one, I really need to hear your best guess as to when we will have definitive data."

3. *Democratic.* This approach uses a process that is very familiar to most members since it involves voting. Here, a decision is proposed and members are asked to vote yes or no to indicate their support or opposition. Majority vote can be used under conditions like these:

- When it is important to record each member's position on an issue.

- When a fast and efficient decision is needed.

- When the leader wants to be certain a majority of the members support a decision.

*Potential Problems*

- Voting often eliminates or minimizes discussion that has the potential of bringing out important views on the topic.

- Voting creates both winners and potentially powerful losers who may impede implementation of the decision and progress on future issues.

- If the voting takes place openly at a meeting (say, with a show of hands), members may feel uncomfortable in being forced to take a public stand.

- Some team members, especially those who voted against the idea, may not fully buy in to the decision.

*Facilitator Comments*
- "The issue on the table is whether we should submit the application as stated in our project plan or delay the submission until this problem is resolved. How many believe we should go forward as planned? How many think we should delay the submission?"

- "Since we need to get back to management by the end of business today, how many people think we should continue as planned? How many think we should delay as proposed by Jeff?"

4. *Expert.* In this case, the decision is delegated to the subject matter expert on the team. It is agreed that this person knows about the issue (and other members know little or nothing about it) and there is little to be gained by involving others in the decision process. In a variation of this method called "consensus with qualification" the team tries to reach a consensus but if it cannot, the member with the most expertise makes the decision with input from other members. In this way, the team can move on rather than be paralyzed by its inability to reach a consensus. There are some obvious situations where the expert approach works well:

- When there is a true expert on the team.

- When the other members acknowledge the expertise of the person.

- When the members accept the fact that they know little or nothing about the issue.

- When the team recognizes a need for a fast and efficient decision.

*Potential Problems*

- Members will feel left out of the decision process.

- Members may question the expertise of the expert.

- Members miss an opportunity to learn something about the topic.

*Facilitator Comments*

- "This is clearly a decision that can only be made by Marketing since the rest of us know little or nothing about the subject."

- "It looks like we are not going to be able to reach a consensus, so let's ask our functional expert, Johan, to take our input and make the decision on behalf of the team."

5. *Averaging (Splitting the Difference).* Some decisions, especially those involving numbers, lend themselves to a compromise answer. If, for example, members propose several amounts to be added to the team's budget, it might be possible to simply compute a mean to obtain a team decision. In situations that do not involve numbers, a decision could be fashioned by taking something from each proposal to create a compromise decision. Another related method involves taking the midpoint ("splitting the difference") between two proposed numbers. This method works in situations like these:

- When the team has several clear alternatives from which to choose.

- When the external stakeholder or customer is willing to accept a compromise.

- When members are willing to abandon their proposals in favor of a new alternative.

- When the alternatives lend themselves to averaging or splitting the difference.

*Potential Problems*
- No one on the team is satisfied with the compromise. ("We have minimized our dissatisfaction" may allow the team to move forward, but if everyone is truly reluctant, efforts to implement the compromise may not be productive.)
- If members seek a compromise to a decision that does not easily lend itself to a compromise, the resulting decision may not work.

*Facilitator Comments*
- "It looks like about a half of the group wants to ask for a $100,000 increase while the rest of you think we can get by with about $50,000; let's split the difference and ask for $75,000."
- "How about if we take Barbra's suggestion of [specific points] and combine that with Robert's proposal of [additional points] and make that our recommendation?"

6. *The Plop.* Some teams make a decision by taking no action. You may have experienced this approach. An issue facing the team is discussed, several alternatives are proposed, but in the end no clear decision is made. Many words are spoken, even some emotion expressed, but at some point, the team moves on to the next agenda item. The decision just "plops."

*Potential Problems*
- Important issues are unresolved.
- Members have different understandings of what happened or what was decided. Some think a decision was made and are clear about what it was without realizing that they disagree with one another, and still others are not sure if anything was decided.
- Valuable team meeting time is wasted.

*Facilitator Comments*

- ◆ "Before we move on, let's get some clarity on how we have decided to handle the issue."

- ◆ "We seem to have moved on to the next agenda item, but I am not clear about what we decided to do about [the preceding one]. Can someone tell me what they believe was decided?"

7. *Consensus.* For important issues, teams often seek a consensus decision. A consensus is an interactive process in which members share their experiences, expertise, and opinion and come to an agreement that everyone can live with. In other words, they understand it and are willing to support and implement the decision although they may not totally agree with all aspects of it. Consensus differs from a unanimous decision in which all members are in complete agreement with the decision. A team should choose this decision method in circumstances like these:

   - When there is no one expert in the room or readily available to the team.

   - When the decision is of some importance to the team.

   - When sufficient time is available. (The consensus process takes longer than other methods.)

   - When no clear answer is available.

   - When no legal, regulatory, or corporate policy mandates a certain outcome.

   - Most important, when commitment on the part of team members to the decision is essential.

   - When there are fewer than 10 members involved in the decision process.

*Potential Problems*

- ◆ When there is not enough time for discussion of the various points of view essential to a real consensus, the process is likely to break down.

♦ When the team climate does not include open communication, members suppress their views on the issue and any appearance of consensus is false.

♦ People assume they have achieved a consensus because no objections are expressed. In reality, there are strong but unspoken concerns about the decision.

♦ When the team is too large to get everyone involved in the discussion required to reach a true consensus.

*Facilitator Comments*

♦ "This is such an important issue that we need to hear everyone's point of view in an effort to reach a team consensus."

♦ "We have discussed this proposal at great length and heard from just about everyone and it looks like we are saying that Market Quest offers the best solution at the present time. Have I stated our consensus accurately?"

♦ "It sounds like some of you have reservations while others don't think it meets all of our needs—but everyone is agreed it is the best way to go and you are all willing work hard to successfully implement it. Is this how you see the situation?"

## Process for Reaching a Consensus

1. *Describe the desired outcome or decision or problem to be solved:* "By the end of this meeting, we need to decide to either continue, change, or drop the ABXY study."

2. *Clarify the decision-making method:* "Because of the importance of this decision, I recommend that we seek a consensus on this issue."

3. *Quickly remind the team about your norms on consensus decision*

*making:* "As you recall, our norms for reaching a consensus include making sure everyone has an opportunity to express their point of view, being willing to listen to and consider all points of view, supporting a decision you can live with even though it does not address all of your concerns, and being willing to support the implementation of the decision."

4. *Begin by asking for a review of the advantages and disadvantages of the options:* "Before we jump to a solution or decision, let's start by discussing the advantages and disadvantages of each option so that we are all clear about what is involved in this decision."

5. *At the appropriate point, test for a possible consensus:* "We've looked at all sides of the issue and it seems to me that we are saying that our recommendation is to terminate the project in 30 days unless the following conditions are met . . ."

6. *If the decision is of great importance, you may want to ensure everyone's commitment by specifically checking with all members:* "Ramon, can you live with it? Joanne, are you in agreement that this is the way to . . . ?" And so on around the group.

7. *Conclude with a list of steps designed to ensure smooth implementation:* "Let's review the action items for this decision and make sure we know who is responsible for each item."

## Related Tools

- Meeting Time Management (tool #12)
- Staying on Track (tool #13)
- How to Get Effective Participation (tool #14)
- Resolving Conflicts in a Team Meeting (tool #21)
- Web-Based Meeting Tools (Resource A)

# 20

# PRESENTING AT A TEAM MEETING

## *Purpose*

Giving a presentation to your colleagues at a team meeting can be either a frightening prospect or a wonderful opportunity, or both! Fortunately, about 90 percent of the result is in your hands. You determine the quality of the content, the usefulness of the slides, the effectiveness of your delivery, and the ease with which you handle the questions.

This tool provides tips for each stage (plus a couple of general segments):

- Preparing the content
- Creating the slides
- Delivering the presentation
- Responding to questions
- Bonus: Recommendations for team presentation
- Bonus: Tips for team facilitators

### Preparing Your Presentation

1. Tips for preparing yourself:

   - *Be audience centered.* What do your teammates want or need to know? Resist the temptation to tell them only what you think they should know. Do they need lots of detail or just an overview? Do they need the history or simply the current situation? Equally important, curb your desire to demonstrate how much you know about the subject.

---

*Note:* This tool draws upon material developed by Marjorie Brody, CSP, CMC, PCC, © 2005 by Marjorie Brody and Brody Communications, Ltd and is used with permission. For more information, go to www.marjorie.brody.com.

- *Have a goal.* What do you want your colleagues to know or to do as a result of your presentation? If you are looking for action or a decision, be clear about it. If you have a clear goal, this will both narrow the scope and provide your presentation with a clear focus.

- *Know the subject.* Nothing takes the place of thorough knowledge of the subject matter. However, if there are things you don't know or areas where you want help from your teammates, be clear about them. One of your goals for the presentation can be to obtain feedback from other members of the team.

- *Make it conversational.* Avoid a formal, stiff presentation; instead, try for an informal, conversational talk appropriate for a gathering of friends. The more you prepare and become comfortable with the content of the presentation, the easier it will be to relax and adopt a conversational style. Since teams tend to be small groups, a conversational style is the best approach.

- *Use examples and stories.* Interesting stories, examples, comparisons, and metaphors can spice up your presentation and make it memorable. You can also use a provocative question or problem situation as an attention-getter.

- *Don't rely on notes.* When you keep referring to notes, you disrupt the flow of the presentation and make it more difficult to speak in a conversational manner. It also means you must look away from the audience. We suggest that you use the content of the slides as your presentation notes. Each bullet item should provide a cue to the substance of the point you want to communicate—but *not* be the text you plan to read. Once again, the more you prepare and practice, the less you will rely on notes.

- *Practice, practice, practice.* The best way to adopt a conversational style, minimize the use of notes, know the subject, and be prepared for audience questions is to practice your presentation.

While a so-called dry run or practice session of your presentation with several of your colleagues is desirable, it is not always possible or even necessary. You can simply review the slides on your computer screen or a print copy while you think about what you want to say and how you want to say it. Some people are even able to visualize themselves delivering the presentation. The method you use is not as important as the fact that you do it. A run-through also helps you adjust to the time allocated to your talk. Practice may not make perfect—but it helps.

2.  Tips for preparing your slides:

    - *Keep it simple.* Generally, the goal is to limit the number of lines and words on a slide. Anytime you have to say, "I know you can't read this," the slide is too busy. If you have a table with a great deal of data presented in very small fonts, for example, it makes no sense to project it on the screen and expect the team to review it in detail. Instead, distribute it as a handout and then discuss it. A good rule of thumb is to limit the number of lines on a slide to five and the number of words per line to six.

    - *Limit the number of slides.* Once you have finished preparing the slides, go back and thoughtfully edit the text to eliminate words and reduce the slide count. Think about you feel when you receive the presentation file for an upcoming presentation at a team meeting and, upon opening the file, find it contains 50 slides! In an obvious reaction to long slide presentations, some teams have a ground rule that limits the number of slides used at a team meeting presentation.

    - *Use one font.* Do not vary the font of the type during the course of a presentation. However, you should make use of upper- and lowercase letters to make it more interesting.

    - *Write attention-getting slide titles.* A slide title such as "A Tale of Two Sites," "Data from Disneyland," or "Well Done!" will evoke interest on the part of your audience. One caution: Don't try to get too cute and clever.

- *Highlight important words and ideas.* Use boldface, italics, or contrasting color to call attention to important words. However, remember that this technique can become distracting and look rather unprofessional; use it sparingly.

- *Carefully select a presentation template.* When you elect to use an existing template, choose one that has dark text on a light background.

- *Use transitions.* A transition that inconspicuously occurs as you move from slide to slide and signals the movement to the next line on a slide is helpful. However, a transition such a "cover down" or "news flash" can be distracting. In general, something like the "dissolve" or "fade down" transition is preferable. Another useful tool is to dim the lines you've covered as you move from one bullet point to the next. This option helps team members focus on the current topic and more easily follow the presentation.

3. Tips for delivering the presentation:

- *Send the slides out before the meeting.* Each team should have a ground rule that covers this behavior but, at minimum, all presentations should reach the team at least three days before the meeting. If the file contains a large number of slides (and we hope it doesn't), highlight the key slides in the e-mail message.

- *Arrive early.* Get to the room before the meeting to check the equipment. (Is the projector there? Is it working?) You will also want to get a feeling for the shape of the room and arrangement of the furniture. Go to the front of the room where you will present, look out, and imagine the room filled with people.

- *Mind your posture.* When you present, try to stand straight, feet slightly apart, and look out at the group. Do not cross your arms over your chest, hold your hands behind your back or in front of your crotch, or put your hands in your pockets. If the group is small (for example, six to eight people) and the climate informal, you may wish to sit down as you deliver the presentation. However, be aware that your energy level may drop while you are seated; monitor yourself to maintain your enthusiasm and interest in the topic.

- *Use effective gestures.* Since the audience at a team meeting tends to be small, hand movements should be minimal and controlled. The best gesture is palms open, up and toward the group. Do not point your finger or clasp your hands together in the prayer position (despite the fact you are actually praying that the presentation will go well and you will not embarrass yourself and your teammates).

- *Look up, look front.* Look around the room at various members of the team as you present. You are checking for signs of interest, comprehension, or boredom. Minimize the times you look back at the wall screen, down at your computer screen, or at your notes.

- *Show your interest in the topic.* If you drone on in a monotone with little animation, you cannot expect your teammates to care about your data, your proposal, or your recommendation. Your facial expression and the tone of your voice combine with your posture and gestures to convey an energetic yet controlled (it *is* still a small-group presentation) interest in the presentation content.

- *Watch your time.* This point may seem obvious, but it bears repeating anyway: if you are given 15 minutes on the agenda, scale your presentation to fit that time slot! A practice session will help here. You do not want to be the person who causes the meeting to run late.

- *End with something.* Don't just let your presentation trail off with "Well, that's all I have to say" or "That's about it." A conclusion need not be long, but it should either quickly review the key points or clearly state your recommendation, plan, or list of next steps (or both). If you are asking the team for something, here is the time to clearly state it. ("A careful analysis of the results, a review of various alternatives, leads me to strongly recommend that we go with Market Quest here.")

4. Tips for handling routine question-and-answer segments:

- *Plan your time.* If questions are an expected part of presentations at your team meetings, make sure you allocate time for your teammates to ask them. If there are no questions, no one will be unhappy if you finish early.

- *Think about what questions are likely to be asked.* Try to anticipate the areas of your talk that will be of most interest to team members, most contentious, or most confusing. Then be prepared for possible questions in these areas.

- *Establish a ground rule.* At the outset of the talk, make it clear to the team when you prefer to take questions: at the end of a section, at the end of the presentation, or whenever they arise.

- *Paraphrase the question.* If the question is couched in a long preface, contains lots of detail, or makes clear how the questioner feels about the issue, paraphrase the essence of the question before responding. Try something like this: "Catherine, if I hear you correctly, you want to know if we have conclusive data about the customer returns. Is that your question?" This technique gives the questioner an opportunity to either agree to or alter the point under discussion, ensures that you understand the question, makes sure the whole audience knows what you're answering, and gives you additional time to formulate your response.

- *Be willing to say, "I don't know."* If you do not know the answer, it is best to simply say, "I don't know, but I will check into it and get back to you as soon as possible." It also may help to offer information about a similar situation, as in "I don't have complete data yet about the customer returns of that product but I do have a final report on the returns of [this related item]."

5. Tips for dealing with hostile questions:

- *Paraphrase the question.* Sometimes just using your active listening skills defuses the hostility. It also gives you time to compose your response.

- *Remain calm.* Provide your response in a calm, professional manner.

- *Be brief.* Hostile questions often come with a great deal of detail, background information, and emotion. Whether or not that is the case, your response should be brief, pointed, and cool; the contrast will help you if the question was overheated, and an overheated response to a cool question will damage your position.

- *Offer to meet privately.* After offering one or at most two responses to the question, suggest that you meet with the questioner at the end of the meeting or at a later time. "Hector, it looks like we need to move on to the next agenda item, but I will be glad to get together with you at the end of the meeting when I can provide more background information on the problem."

6. Tips for team presentations:

- *Select a team leader or facilitator.* For an effective presentation, you need one person to be responsible for facilitating the preparation process, introducing the presentation, and managing the question-and-answer period.

- *Limit the number of presenters.* While it is tempting to include all members of a team in an effort to be inclusive and democratic, rarely should a session have more than four presenters. It can get confusing and distracting for the audience if they have to adjust to a wider variety of speaking styles.

- *Divide responsibilities.* Clearly delineate the topics that each presenter will cover. You want connections and transitions between the sections but not duplication. You do not want the overall session to appear uncoordinated and therefore, unprofessional.

- *Use the same template.* Agree on a presentation template and then insist that all the presenters use it. Similarly, all the slides should use the same transitions and animations.

- *Plan the transitions between speakers.* Will the team leader introduce the sections and the speakers? Will each speaker introduce the next section and the next speaker? Will the speakers each do their own personal and topic introductions? Any of these approaches can be effective. However, the whole presentation should use the same transition style.

- *Hold a team practice.* For a major presentation, plan to hold at least one practice session with all the speakers. If possible, ask some other team members to attend as observers and to provide feedback.

- *Agree on the question ground rule.* Will you take questions at the end of each section or only at the end of the total presentation? Will the team leader take the question and hand it off to the appropriate person? Will the speakers take the question directly if it appears to be about their section?

- *Have the leader provide a summary.* At the end of the presentation, including the question-and-answer period, the leader should offer a summary and possible next steps.

7. Tips for the meeting facilitator:

- *Introduce the presentation.* You should introduce the presentation by providing the context. Clarify the purpose of the presentation, the expected outcome or next steps, and the time allocated to the presentation.

- *Manage the time.* By arrangement, provide the presentation team leader with hand signals that indicate the amount of time remaining.

- *Intervene.* You may stop the presentation when you sense confusion about a specific topic. Say something like, "Ralph, there appears to be some question about your approach to this problem. Let's stop here and see if you can answer a few of these questions. Jennifer, am I right that you have a question?" You may also intervene if you believe there will not be enough time for the last speaker or the question-and-answer period. Try something like this: "I am concerned that we will not have enough time for Jackson's presentation on the impact. So, let's wrap this up in the next few minutes and move on."

- *Manage hostility.* If you see that the speaker is unable to handle a hostile questioner, you may intervene to cut off the questioner. ("Ingrid, I suggest that you meet with Jacques after the meeting to continue this discussion because we have to move to the next section now.") Alternatively, you may elect to continue the discussion of the topic but allow other people to join the conversation. ("I think we have heard how Ingrid feels about this; let's get some other opinions from the rest of you.")

**Related Tools**

- Preparing for Your Next Meeting (tool #2)
- How to Prepare an Action Agenda (tool #3)
- Staying on Track (tool #13)
- How to Get Effective Participation (tool #14)
- Managing Meeting Monsters (tool #23)

# 21

# RESOLVING CONFLICTS IN A TEAM MEETING

## *Purpose*

Conflicts are endemic to team meetings. Effective teams expect them, even welcome them. If you define conflicts as *differences* or *disagreements,* then it's easy to see them as a natural part, a positive aspect of the team meeting landscape. In fact, one could say that if a meeting does not include any potential differences among members, why bother to meet? But nonetheless, conflicts are often viewed as negative because of the inability of the team to *resolve* them effectively.

Conflicts in team meetings usually center on one or more of these elements:

- *Decisions.* These are differences about what the team should do. Should we add three more salespeople to the region? Should we enter into an agreement with Market Quest?

- *Direction.* Disagreements in this area focus on strategic issues that deal with where the team should be heading. Should we expand our scope of work to include Asia/Pacific? Should we forge a development partnership with Hoffpark?

- *Priorities.* Arguments here are usually about the relative importance of issues, tasks, or other project components. In these conflicts, a not-so-hidden agenda may be how the funds will be distributed. Should our two new members be assigned to reshape the marketing plan? Should we divert funds allocated to ABC to improve the XYZ area?

- *Process.* At times people clash over how the team should approach an issue. Should we empower the development team to make the decision for us? Should we throw out the rest of the agenda and just work on this issue until we reach a consensus?

- *Expectations.* At some team meetings conflicts arise when members have different expectations of each other. Often these clashes result from lack of clarity about roles ("Isn't Technical Operations supposed to do that?"), although they sometimes come from personality or style differences ("Why are you so impatient with our progress?").

The purpose of this tool is to provide facilitators and members with tips for effective conflict resolution.

## Tips for Meeting Facilitators

- *Manage the process.* First, be clear about your process and then help the participants follow it. If, for example, you want to be sure of achieving clarity about points of view, be sure that the participants state their positions without jumping to a solution.

- *Don't deny or smooth over differences.* Over time, if you deny the existence of a conflict ("There is no problem with MP") or minimize it ("It's nothing serious"), the issues will remain just below the surface. Unresolved conflict can erupt at inappropriate times (at the end of a long meeting) or at inappropriate forums (a project review with senior management). It is your role as meeting facilitator to help the team address these issues.

- *Ensure understanding.* Ask everyone to indicate their own position ("I want to discontinue the brand development project with Market Quest"). Explore the reasons behind the position. Use active listening and open-ended questions like these to get to a thorough understanding:

  "Why is this change necessary?"

  "What can you tell us about your experience with this issue?"

  "What are the biggest concerns?"

  "So you are saying that Market Quest has not delivered on its promises?"

"In other words, you feel that Market Quest has not been given sufficient time to fulfill its obligations?"

- *Be supportive and encouraging.* Indicate that you understand why people are concerned about the issue, why they feel so strongly about it, and that it is a legitimate concern. In all this, you are not indicating that you support or oppose either side.

- *Clarify the alternatives.* Help the participants develop a set of possible solutions. Be careful at this stage of the tendency to "split the difference." When you compromise by agreeing to a middle ground, it usually does not solve the problem and leaves both sides feeling dissatisfied. Rather you are looking here for a list of viable options that are real solutions to the conflict. In many conflict situations, seeking alternatives may require the group to step back and imagine new possibilities rather than accepting one of the initial proposals or jumping for traditional solutions.

- *Avoid jumping to a single solution.* Resist the tendency to get into a discussion that focuses solely on the advantages and disadvantages of just one answer. More creative solutions result from an examination of a range of possibilities. Sometimes, what begins as a crazy idea can be shaped into an innovative outcome.

- *Consider a pilot program.* If team members cannot reach a consensus on a permanent solution, propose a pilot or trial plan with a limited time frame and specific evaluation criteria. "Let's set up a three-month trial with Market Quest, at the end of which we will evaluate the extent to which they have signed up the required number of customers."

- *Break the problem into manageable parts.* If you cannot come to a resolution of the total problem, consider slicing and dicing the issue into smaller parts. "Since we can't seem to agree on a global solution, let's develop one plan for Europe, one for Asia/Pacific, and another for Africa."

- *Defuse anger.* If meeting participants become angry and speak to each other in disrespectful ways, immediate action on your part is required. Some possible responses:

  - Stop the discussion, indicating that this is not appropriate behavior.

  - Take a short break to allow the participants to cool off.

  - Review the relevant team norms dealing with such behaviors as respect, being open to new ideas, avoiding personal attacks, and practicing active listening.

  - Remind the participants about the need to present usable ideas rather than just attack the other person's ideas.

  - Revisit the goal of the discussion: to come up with a solution that is best for the team, the project, and the company. The goal is not to win a victory for any specific solution.

## Tips for Meeting Participants

- *Remember that the goal is a win-win outcome.* In any conflict, the goal is not to have your solution to become the team's solution. The goal is to resolve the conflict in a way that is best for the team (that is, that supports the team's goals).

- *Be open to alternatives.* Keep an open mind. There may be data that you have not seen, opinions you have not heard, and solutions you have not considered.

- *Use active listening.* Sometimes a perceived conflict is not a conflict at all but a failure to communicate. For various reasons you may not completely understand the situation, especially the ideas presented by other team members. In that case, when you stop and paraphrase what the person is proposing, it may just be that you agree. And where the disagreement is real, developing a clear understanding of the positions of other members is the first step toward conflict resolution.

- *Steer clear of either-or arguments.* It is rare that a creative outcome will emerge from a discussion that focuses solely on debating the merits of "my" solution versus "your" solution. In that situation, look for a solution that combines some of each idea with other ideas.

- *Refrain from personal attacks.* In a conflict the discussion is about ideas, opinions, and data. It should not be a forum for attacking the credibility of the person presenting the ideas.

- *Be willing to live with a consensus.* In the end the most effective resolution to a conflict may be a consensus that meets some but not all of your concerns. Be willing to support such an outcome.

## Related Tools

- Establishing Your Team's Ground Rules (tool #7)
- How to Get Effective Participation (tool #14)
- Building a Foundation of Trust (tool #15)
- Achieving Clear Communication in a Multicultural Meeting (tool #18)
- How to Make a Decision (tool #19)
- Responding to Nonverbal Communication (tool #22)
- Managing Meeting Monsters (tool #23)

# 22

# RESPONDING TO NONVERBAL COMMUNICATION

## *Purpose*

Some experts say that nonverbal communication accounts for about 80 percent of the meaning in face-to-face interactions. And, more important, since most nonverbal behaviors are involuntary, they usually express the person's real feelings. The problem is that we concentrate so much on the spoken word that we miss most of the nonverbal messages sent our way. Perhaps even more significant is the fact that we often misread the intent of the few nonverbal messages that do come to our attention. So, as a meeting facilitator, what can you do?

First, some background on what we are talking about. Nonverbal messages are typically sent via one or the other of these channels:

- *Facial expressions.* Making eye contact, raising an eyebrow, smiling, frowning, squinting, looking up, looking down, and other expressions may be cues to what a team member is thinking—and, in fact, wants to communicate to you.

- *Body positions and movements.* Leaning forward, leaning back, pushing away from the table, sitting with arms folded or arms open wide, turning away or to one side, nodding, and making other movements may signal the person's real intentions.

Second, consider these team meeting scenarios:

1. Maria is sitting in a meeting that you are leading. At the conclusion of a presentation, she folds her arms across her chest. What is she communicating by this action?

2. As another member is making a point about the current agenda item, Rolf is looking upward, not making eye contact with the speaker. What is he communicating by this action?

3. At the end of the meeting you review the decisions made by the team during the meeting. As you are going through the list, you notice Anna nodding her head up and down. What does this mean?

At the end of this tool, you will find possible answers to these questions about the meaning of nonverbal cues. In the meantime, think about how you would interpret the actions if you were facilitating the meeting.

**Tips for Responding to Nonverbal Communication**

- *Be aware.* As you approach your next meeting, keep in mind that all this nonverbal communication is taking place. Notice, but don't respond to, various cues expressed by meeting participants. It is helpful to develop a sensitivity to nonverbal behaviors before you begin responding in any way.

- *Stop, don't assume.* Approach people with caution; you can never be sure you fully understand the meaning of their nonverbal actions. Asserting that you know what someone is thinking from their nonverbal behavior may be seen as arrogant. And if you are wrong, it will be a major setback to your relationship with this person as well as with other team members.

- *Look for consistent responses.* It is usually not necessary to respond the first time you notice a specific nonverbal cue. However, if you become aware that the person consistently responds in a particular way in similar situations, you may consider responding in some way. ("Marco, if I am reading you correctly, it seems as if you are not comfortable with the way we are moving on this issue. Is that true?")

- *Look for patterns.* If you see several members responding nonverbally to a presentation, something significant may be happening. If you observe negative reactions such as heads moving side to side, or people pushing back from the table or rolling their eyes, you can tentatively assume that there are some significant disagreements with or questions about this presentation. Your response might be to intervene with something like, "Gina, let me stop you here because I sense people have some questions about what you have said so far." You can then ask an overhead question to the whole group or use a direct question to one of the nonverbal responders. ("Does anyone have questions or comments for Gina?" or "Roberto, do you have some questions about what has been said thus far?")

- *Make it a question.* Since you can never be sure your interpretation of the nonverbal behavior is accurate, it is always best to approach the person with a question. A question gives the person an opportunity to disagree ("No, Glenn, I have no problems with what has been said") or to join the discussion ("Yes, Glenn, as a matter of fact, I think we are moving in the wrong direction on this issue").

Here are possible interpretations of the three scenarios introduced at the beginning of this tool:

**Interpreting Team Meeting Scenarios**

1. Maria is sitting in a meeting that you are leading. At the conclusion of a presentation, she folds her arms across her chest. What is she communicating by this action?

   - *Maria has closed her mind and is not open to any new ideas on this subject.*

   - *Maria is saying, "It's cold in this room. Why don't they cut back the air conditioning?"*

2. As another member is making a point about the current agenda item, Rolf is looking upward, not making eye contact with the speaker. What is he communicating by this action?

- *Rolf is not interested in what is being said.*
- *Rolf is giving serious thought to what is being said.*

3. At the end of the meeting you review the decisions made by the team during the meeting. As you are going through the list, you notice Anna nodding her head up and down. What does this mean?

   - *Anna agrees with what you are saying.*
   - *Anna is simply listening to what you are saying.*

Since each of these interpretations is possible, the exercise is a reminder of the difficulty of correctly understanding nonverbal behaviors. It also reinforces the importance of looking for patterns and consistency—and, most important, couching your response as a question rather than a flat statement that may well be wrong.

**Related Tools**

- How to Get Effective Participation (tool #14)
- Building a Foundation of Trust (tool #15)
- Communicating in a Videoconference (tool #16)
- Achieving Clear Communication in a Multicultural Meeting (tool #18)
- Managing Meeting Monsters (tool #23)

# 23

## MANAGING MEETING MONSTERS

### *DEALING WITH DIFFICULT BEHAVIOR IN TEAM MEETINGS*

## *Purpose*

Sometimes all your best efforts as a meeting leader just do not work. Sometimes the negative actions of a member of the team make it extremely difficult for you to achieve the objectives of the meeting. You build a great agenda, assemble all the documents and people, and even start on time, but during the meeting a member of the team engages in some type of dysfunctional behavior. Our purpose here is to provide you with an array of tools to address the behavior and get the meeting back on track.

To set the stage, here are some typical meeting monsters that can derail a meeting:

- *Silent Sara.* The silent ones sit through the meeting without saying a word, often giving the impression of not wanting to be there. In addition, their nonverbal behavior—arms crossed and lips tight—reinforces their silence.

- *Monopolizer Manfried.* Monopolizers love the sound of their own voice. As a result, they feel the need to speak on every topic, often at length. They are close cousins to the Verbose Victoria type, people who love words, especially their own, and believe that more is better than less.

- *Sidetalkers Sanji and Suzanne.* Characters like these two disrupt the communication flow of the meeting by engaging in ongoing side conversations. Their behavior is especially troublesome in a videoconference, where additional noise is very distracting.

- *Negative Nelson.* The Negative Nelsons of the world are full-time contrarians who dislike everything and everyone and never contribute a positive or supportive thought. They are second cousins to the Argumentative Als, who run toward rather than away from a good (or bad) fight. Nelson and Al should not be confused with the Challenger Charley types, who raise difficult but important issues for the team to consider.

- *Tangent Tanya.* These people have many ideas on many topics but rarely are these ideas related to the agenda item under discussion. They enjoy taking the team down a path that leads the group away from the key meeting outcome.

- *Condescending Clarissa.* This type of person is often arrogant, impatient, and disdainful of other members of the team, especially of their subject matter knowledge. At times, they can be mocking and demonstrate a lack of respect for their teammates.

Before we provide you with some tools to address the negative behaviors that you encounter in your meetings, it's useful to understand the key types.

## Tips for Dealing with Difficult Behavior

- *Focus on behavior.* Resist the temptation to focus on problem people. It is important to stay focused the behavior and not on the meeting monsters, their personalities, or their attitudes. That's why this section is not titled "Tips for Dealing with Problem People." It is more productive and much easier to alter disruptive behavior than to change the personality or style of a member.

- *Look for a pattern of behavior.* Sitting silently through one meeting or becoming argumentative about one agenda item is not a cause for action. You only need to act when the behavior occurs several times over the course of more than a few meetings.

- *Listen with an open mind.* It may be that the person has a point or is raising an issue that you need to consider. What you think of as dysfunctional behavior may just be a different style—and your inability to appreciate it. What you see as Argumentative Al may just be Challenger Charley trying to stop the team from making a bad choice. What you see as a Tangent Tanya acting up may just be someone doing some necessary thinking outside boundaries that may be unnecessarily restricting the team. So take a deep breath and consider the value of the contribution rather than quickly labeling the speaker as a difficult person.

- *Then react with an open mind.* Instead of responding with something like "Your comment tells me you don't understand the issue or you did not read the project report," try this: "Help me understand why you think this new approach will solve the data problem." As an alternative to attacking the person who sits quietly through meetings as a "non team player," try asking the person if there is something about the meeting process that could be changed to make it easier to participate.

- *Reestablish or refocus on team norms.* If the behavior in question is addressed in one of your ground rules, facilitate a discussion on the norms that focuses on the extent to which the team is adhering to them, their current relevance, and any new norms that may be needed. A discussion of norms should encourage the members who have violated them to change their behavior and encourage other members to provide feedback to people who consistently breach the norms. See tool #7, "Establishing Your Team's Ground Rules."

- *Meet privately.* If the behavior continues over time, ask to meet with the person after the meeting, face to face or, if necessary, by phone. Try something like this: "Sanji, may I have a few minutes of your time to discuss a concern I have about the way our team meeting is going?" Remember to focus on their behavior and the impact on team meeting effectiveness. "Sanji, during the past three meetings both you and

Suzanne regularly engage in private side conversation while other team members are presenting their reports or commenting on agenda items. The net result is that it is difficult to hear what other people are saying and you appear to not be interested in the discussion. It also shows a lack of respect for your teammates. I wonder if you are aware of how this behavior impacts the team and the overall effectiveness of the meeting." At this point encourage Sanji to respond with his perception of the situation. Your goal here is to get an agreement to change the behavior. Two techniques you can use:

- *Negotiation.* Sometimes you can neutralize dysfunctional behavior by negotiating an informal agreement with the person where you change something about how to lead the meeting in exchange for an agreement to alter the negative behavior. For example, the outcome may require that you change some aspect of your meeting process, such as increasing the pace of the meeting or scheduling a break during the meeting if the team member agrees to minimize the side conversations.

- *Positive reinforcement.* When the person who has been engaging in the negative behavior changes or makes a positive contribution, provide positive feedback. For example, when Once-Condescending Clarissa is supportive and encouraging of another member, say something like, "Thanks, Clarissa, I'm pleased that you found Marianne's report helpful. I'm sure Marianne also appreciated your comments because she put a great deal of effort into the preparation of the report."

• *Be prepared for a confrontation.* Although it is best to talk with the person privately, sometimes it is necessary to confront the behavior during the meeting when it happens. As in a private conversation, it is important to be specific, focus on behavior, and point out the impact on the meeting. For example, "Al, your persistence in insisting that we conduct additional studies at this time is slowing us down and causing us to miss a critical deadline and upset senior management."

Dealing with difficult behavior in meetings is difficult. Therefore, carefully consider these things before you take any action.

- What are consequences of doing nothing? Consider the degree of difficulty involved in trying to change the behavior versus the impact on the team of allowing the behavior to continue.

- Plan, prepare, and then plan and prepare some more. Take the time to think about the behavior, the person, how you will approach and engage the person, and your goal for the intervention.

- Focus on the behavior. Be specific about the actions that are dys-functional (consistently coming late to the meeting) and the impact on the meeting (we need your input on issues that are discussed before you arrive).

- Give the person an opportunity to respond. Consider the fact that the person may have a different perception of the behavior. ("I'm stuck with a regular meeting that ends when this one is set to begin; it's in another building and the travel time is 20 min-utes at a minimum.")

- Don't be a street-corner psychologist. It is not helpful to offer your view of the motivation for the person's behavior. ("Coming late to our team meeting is a passive-aggressive way of telling me you really don't want to be here" is unlikely to inspire whole-hearted support for the team's work.) Similarly, interpreting a person's nonverbal behavior can be just as destructive ("The fact that you sat through most of the meeting with your arms folded across your chest tells me you had already made up your mind and were not open to the new approach proposed by Anthony" will greatly irritate a team member with a bellyache or a chill.)

**Related Tools**

- Staying on Track (tool #13)
- How to Get Effective Participation (tool #14)
- Communicating in a Videoconference (tool #16)
- Teleconference Tips (tool #17)
- How to Make a Decision (tool #19)
- Responding to Nonverbal Communication (tool #22)

# 24

## SERIOUS FUN AT TEAM MEETINGS?

*YOU'RE KIDDING!*

## *Purpose*

Most team meetings deal with serious business. Challenging deadlines must be met. Difficult scientific and technical issues must be addressed. Government regulations require plans for compliance. And very often, the team faces the challenge of communicating across cultures, time zones, and balky technology.

So, in this context, can you have fun at a team meeting and still meet your objectives? The answer is yes—but it requires careful planning and may mean taking some reasonable risks.

In the end, fun has a serious purpose. The desired outcome of fun is an informal, relaxed climate in a meeting. In such a climate, people do their best problem solving and decision making. Communication is more likely to be direct and clear. And creative solutions and innovative plans are more likely to emerge.

Here are some options:

- *Food.* Food, even small snacks, can help create a relaxed climate. But don't stop at coffee, tea, and pastry. This is standard meeting food and typically not much fun, unless, of course, you add a fun element to it. The goal: make it fun by making it something that participants will talk about.

- *Personal activities.* Any activity that helps team members get to know each other better can be fun for everyone and improve interpersonal communication. The goal: short, easy-to-use, and playful tools that help team members get to know each other better as people rather than just by role or expertise (scientist, sales rep) so as to build a more informal, relaxed atmosphere that fosters open communication and a higher level of trust.

- *Games.* Playful activities can teach concepts, convey information, and provide opportunities to practice important skills. You want games that are short, easy to understand, and applicable to a multicultural team environment. You may wish to provide small prizes to winners or to everyone who completes the game. The goal: demonstrate something significant about teamwork—and, of course, be fun.

- *Toys.* Small toys relieve stress, provide a needed break, encourage creativity, and are just plain fun. The goal: enliven a dreary group, defuse a potential conflict situation, loosen up a stressful meeting, and, of course, add a little fun to a normally serious group.

The purpose of this tool is to provide suggestions, guidelines, and resources for adding some fun to your team meetings.

## Food Tips

- *Member's choice.* Instead of ordering typical cafeteria pastry, ask a couple of people to bake their favorite cake, pie, small pastry, or cookies and bring them to the meeting. Rotate the assignment among all members.

- *Chocolate explosion.* Provide all chocolate items such as cookies, brownies, cake, candy, and pudding along with hot and cold chocolate drinks. (Check first to make sure no one on the team hates or is allergic to chocolate!)

- *Ethnic food.* When the meeting is composed of people from different cultures, the food provided can represent those cultures. Ask one of the members to plan the menu. Rotate the responsibility so that the foods of all cultures on the team are presented. The food need only be snacks to be effective.

- *Healthy alternative.* Provide an all-healthy-snack table with fruits, vegetables, yogurt, nuts, juices, and other similar food and drink. It will certainly provoke conversation among members, especially if the food contrasts with unhealthy items served at past meetings.

- *Team Cuisine.* Conclude a face-to-face meeting with team members that includes planning and preparing their own dinner. This event requires advance menu planning and the cooperation of the food service staff. Give some team members responsibility for preparing the menu items (salad, dessert) and others related chores such as setting the table and selecting the wine.

- *Picnic with a purpose.* When the weather is fine, move your meeting outdoors to a nearby park. Provide typical picnic food that you bring with you (such as sandwiches) or prepare easily in the park (hamburgers).

- *Food role reversal.* This idea works well in a global meeting when members are in different countries and attending via videoconference. Reverse the typical snacks provided in each country. For example, serve bagels to the group in England and scones to the people at the site in the United States.

## Personal Activity Tips

- *The Truth.* In this activity, members introduce themselves by telling their teammates five personal things that may not be known to everyone. The items can be drawn from past experiences, hobbies or interests, likes or dislikes, family background, or accomplishments. However, one of the five items presented is not true, though it could be true. The task of the rest of the group is to guess which of the five items is not true.

- *The Newspaper Interview.* Team members are asked to select another person on the team that they do not know well. Each person interviews the chosen subject with the goal of collecting enough information for an introduction to the rest of the team. Interviewers are encouraged to collect information about business and professional life as well as hobbies, interests, and family life. Each interviewer, in turn, introduces their subject beginning with "I would like to introduce [name] and tell you something about [her/him]." The idea behind this exercise is that people are less likely to be modest about one another's accomplishments than about their own, so the whole team will learn more about the value of each member than anyone would volunteer in a self-introduction.

- *What's in a Name?* This activity uses a brief questionnaire to find out interesting information about a person's name. You can prepare a copy of the questions prior to the meeting and distribute it to all members before the meeting. Then simply ask them to introduce themselves using these questions and their answers as a guide.

---

**WHAT'S IN A NAME?**

1. What is your full name?

2. What are some aspects of your family history associated with your name?

3. Do you have a nickname now? What was your nickname as a child?

4. What would like to be called if you could have another name or a nickname? As a child, did you want to have another name?

5. What interesting experiences have you had associated with your name?

---

- *You Are Unforgettable.* Give the group a few minutes to think about and identify one or two things about themselves that are unforgettable (for example, "I ran the New York City Marathon," "I speak six languages," "I collect spiders," "I once had dinner with Sophia Loren"). Then ask each person to talk to a person they do not know very well telling the other person something unforgettable about themselves. Repeat this exercise with several partners. Conclude this activity by asking the group to recall some unforgettable things they were told by other members.

- *I Know Someone Famous.* Ask members of the group to think of some connection they have with a famous person. The connection can be remote or even somewhat ridiculous: "I was on a supermarket check-out line with Walter Cronkite," or "One night I had dinner in the same restaurant as Martin Luther King," or "I went to the same university as Jacques Cousteau." Ask members to introduce themselves to the group including their connection to a famous person.

- *Mystery Guest.* In an e-mail message before the meeting or on a small card passed out at the beginning of the meeting, ask everyone to submit an interesting or unusual fact about themselves (see the two preceding activities for examples). Then the leader reads the cards and the rest of the team tries to guess the name of the "mystery guest" (that is, each team member in turn).

- *Baby Face.* Before the meeting ask each of the members to lend you one of their baby pictures. You can bring the pictures to the meeting, post them on the team space, or in some other way transmit them to the members of the team without identifying the people. At the meeting, ask the members write to their guesses on the identity of the pictures on a slip of paper. After each person has been correctly identified, ask the members to tell the group what other people have told them they were like as a baby.

**Games Tips**

- *Chunks.* In this game a sentence has been cut up into three-character chunks, including spaces and punctuation marks. The team's task is to rearrange the chunks to form the original sentence. The team is to work together to solve the puzzle. The game can be made competitive by creating subteams to work together against other teams. Here are some hints you can offer the group if people run into difficulty:

  ◆ The sentence describes an important principle of teamwork.

  ◆ Locate the chunk that contains a period. This should the last chunk.

  ◆ Any chunk that begins with a space is the beginning of a new word.

  ◆ If you find a chunk that looks like the beginning of a word (but does not have a space in front), this could be the first word in the sentence.

**SAMPLE CHUNKS PUZZLE**

| IN | TE | " I " | AM | IS | NO | RE | THE |

- *Team Quote.* The purpose of this activity is to agree on a quote that best represents your team. Before the meeting prepare copies of the list of quotes in the following box. Distribute the lists and ask each person to do two things before discussing it with anyone else: select the quote that best represents the team now, and guess which quote will get the most votes (that is, be selected) by the members at this meeting. Review the list of quotes and ask for a show of hands (or verbal response) as to who selected each quote. Tally the results. Ask which members selected the winner and why they selected it. You may also ask about differences between the selected choices and the winner. If time permits, you can facilitate a discussion using questions such as these:

- Why is this (quote) important for our team?
- Can you provide some examples of how this works on our team?
- What happens when this factor is not present?
- Which quote would you like to have represent us in the future?

---

### TEAM QUOTES

"Yesterday ended last night."

"Success is getting up one more time than you fall."

"You always have time for things you put first."

"In great attempts, it is glorious even to fail."

"Even if you are on the right track, you'll get run over if you just sit there."

"Nothing of importance was ever done without a plan."

"If the going gets easy, you may be going downhill."

*Source:* S. Thiagarajan and G. Parker, *Teamwork and Team Play*, San Francisco: Jossey-Bass, 1999.

---

- *Brain Games.* Here are a few brief problems that you can use to have some fun at the beginning of a meeting or at break time to refresh the group. You can use the problems one at a time. You make also make it competitive by creating subteams to work together and with the goal of solving the problem first.

  - How can you take one from nineteen and still have twenty?
  - A boy was offered a bonus if he sold one hundred subscriptions to a magazine. Each day he sold three subscriptions more than

he had on the previous day, and on the eighth day he reached his one hundred quota. *How many subscriptions did he sell each day?*

♦ Name ten cities starting with the letter "M" that have more than a million people living in them, *only one city per country.*

♦ Unscramble these letters and make one word from them: OER-WNDO.

♦ Name parts of the body spelled with four letters. *No slang, abbreviations, or plurals.* The team that names the most parts is the winner.

♦ Name the child of the following parents:

Mr. & Mrs. Voyant

Mr. & Mrs. Tress

Mr. & Mrs. Nasium

Mr. & Mrs. Tate

Mr. & Mrs. Five

Mr. & Mrs. Itosis

Mr. & Mrs. Anthemum

Mr. & Mrs. Mander

Mr. & Mrs. Mite

You may need to provide a hint by giving the answer to the first one: "Clare."

---

### ANSWERS

1. Use roman numerals: XIX and XX.

2. First day sales were 2 subscriptions, then 5, 8, 11, 14, 17, 20, and 23, which total 100.

3. Miami, Mexico City, Milan, Moscow, Melbourne, Manila, Madrid, Manchester, Montreal, Montevideo, Madras, Medellín, Marseilles, and Munich.

4. One Word.

5. Nose, hair, neck, vein, skin, heel, palm, brow, calf, nail, bone, pore, drum, jowl, iris, head, chin, face, head, chin, face, cell, arch, nape, anus, lung, knee, lobe, back, uvea, fist, lash, and axon.

6. Clare, Matt, Jim, Dick, Hy, Hal, Chris, Sally, and Dinah.

All of the games in this section are reprinted with permission of Sterling Publishing Co., Inc., NY, NY from **BRAIN BAFFLERS** by Robert Steinwachs, © 1993 by Robert Steinwachs.

- *Murder Mystery.* Prior to the meeting, prepare copies of the mystery case for distribution to the members. Form subteams to compete to get the right answer.

  Read the following story and see if you can figure out the answer to the question.

## THE CASE OF THE ARCTIC EXPLORER

Sir James Harvey, aged bachelor and famed explorer of the North Pole, was found murdered in his bedroom.

The $4,000,000 in thousand-dollar bills, which he was known to keep in his wall safe, was missing.

The police concluded that the criminal or criminals had concealed the money in the house, perhaps in something brought along for the purpose, expecting to recover it later.

This surmise was founded upon Sir James's eccentric precautions. A visitor might gain admission to his estate unchallenged. But no one, including the servants, could leave without being passed by a series of private guards.

On the day Sir James's possessions were put up for auction, Dr. Haledjian joined Sheriff Monahan in the explorer's museum.

"The sale starts here," said the sheriff. "But every stick in the house will be sold today or tomorrow."

An auctioneer had begun to enumerate for the buyers the museum's objects, describing them as Sir James's favorite mementos of his five trips to the Arctic.

The objects included a group of stuffed animals, two polar bears and a penguin, three stuffed fish, and an assortment of Eskimo clothing, utensils, and weapons.

"The murderer has to be in the house," said the sheriff. "But my men can't watch all the rooms."

"Rest at ease," said Haledjian. "He or an accomplice is in this room, ready to make a purchase."

*How did Haledjian know?*

---

### Answer

Haledjian realized the criminal had hidden the money in his own prop—the one thing in the museum that didn't belong with the collection of North Pole objects. The stuffed penguin.

The criminal forgot that penguins live at the South, not the North, Pole!

*Source:* D. Sobol, *Still More Two-Minute Mysteries*, New York: Scholastic, 1975.

---

- *Alphabet Soup.* You can create a quick game that will increase the knowledge base of the members. Simply prepare a list of the abbreviations of various organizations, groups, and boards that are relevant to the team (for example, FDA and ECOM). List the initials in the left column with blank spaces across in the right column. Give a prize to the first person who correctly names all of the organizations. If time permits, facilitate a discussion on the role and responsibilities of each group.

**Tips for Toys**

- *What to choose.* Many kinds of toys will work. Just be sure to introduce them judiciously and with some forethought, and not so often as to overwhelm the business of the meeting. The following suggestions have all been used successfully:

    - Soft squeeze rubber balls

    - Multicolored Koosh balls and Nerf balls

    - Slinky spring toys and similar kinesthetic learning tools

    - Small challenge toys such as Rubik's Cubes, yo-yos, juggling balls, or wooden cups with a ball on a string

    - Small noisemakers such as train whistles or plastic clapping hands

- *Ways to use toys:*

    - Use the balls to facilitate participation by tossing a ball to the next person on the agenda, to a person who wants to add something to the discussion, or to someone whose opinion you want to hear.

    - Use the noisemakers to give positive feedback to a team member who has just completed a presentation or made a positive contribution to the discussion.

    - Use any of the toys as a reward for a team member who makes a positive contribution to the team.

    - Distribute the challenge toys during breaks to recharge the mental energy of the group.

- ◆ Use the toys just for fun. Get to the meeting early. Place a toy at each place around the table or simply put them in a group in the middle of the table and see what happens.
- *Sources for meeting toys:* The two best sources are
  - ◆ www.trainerswarehouse.com
  - ◆ www.creativelearningtools.com

## Related Tools

- Preparing for Your Next Meeting (tool #2)
- Components of a New Team Kick-Off Meeting (tool #8)
- Planning an Off-Site Meeting That's On Target (tool #9)
- How to Get Effective Participation (tool #14)
- Communicating in a Videoconference (tool #16)
- How to Make a Decision (tool #19)
- Eating Well = Meeting Well (tool #25)

# 25

# EATING WELL = MEETING WELL

## *Purpose*

We all talk about the drop-off in energy levels in meetings after the midday meal. To a considerable extent this phenomenon is caused by the type of food consumed at lunch and the degree to which we refresh ourselves during the break. In general, effectiveness in meetings is influenced by the food the participants eat and the amount of movement they engage in during the meeting and during breaks. Sitting for a long time and consuming certain foods may cause a loss in concentration and mental effectiveness.

The purpose of this tool is to suggest a variety of healthy foods and simple exercises designed to keep meeting participants both fit and engaged. Of course, providing food at a team meeting is not a requirement for a successful meeting—but it can help, if you choose the right foods and avoid the wrong ones.

We have grouped our food suggestions around some typical meeting formats. Once again, in suggesting these foods and drinks, we are not implying that all these items should be offered at every meeting.

### Early-Morning Meetings
- Fresh fruit platter with cut pineapple, melon, berries, and oranges.
- Fruit salad made with fresh fruit.
- Individual low-fat yogurt containers.
- Bagels with low-fat butter, cream cheese, and natural fruit spreads.
- Low-fat muffins (*not* doughnuts or pastries).
- 100 percent fruit juices.
- Fat-free milk and fat-free creamer for coffee and tea.

- Low-fat granola and individual boxes of healthy cereals (low sugar, high fiber).
- Herbal and other healthy teas such as green tea, with honey.

## Lunch Meetings

- Green salad with fresh vegetables and low-fat dressing on the side.
- Whole-grain bread and rolls.
- Platter with several types of turkey (smoked, pepper) and low-fat cheeses (Swiss, Jarlsberg) for sandwiches.
- Platter of sandwich condiments such as lettuce, tomatoes, onion, pickles, and olives.
- Spinach salad with fresh fruit, almonds, and low-fat dressing. (No bacon!)
- Whole wheat pasta salad with fresh vegetables and low-fat dressing.
- Platter of cold chicken—grilled, skinned, and sliced—with vegetables and low-fat dressing.
- Tuna salad made with a small amount of mayo or low-fat mayo.
- Chicken salad with grapes and walnuts made with a small amount of mayo or low-fat mayo.
- Turkey chili.
- Vegetable pizza made with whole wheat dough (if available) and fresh tomatoes.
- Taco salad with sliced chicken and low-fat dressing.

## Breaks

- 100 percent fruit juices.
- Fresh fruit platter with low-fat yogurt dip.
- Fresh vegetable platter with low-fat salad dressing dip.

- Low-fat tortilla chips with fresh tomato salsa.
- Healthy snacks such as sourdough pretzels, hot pretzels with mustard, and air-popped (or low-fat microwave) popcorn.
- Oatmeal raisin cookies.
- Sunbelt brand low-fat oatmeal raisin granola bars.
- Bowl of fresh whole fruit such as apples, bananas, pears, plums, oranges, and grapes.
- Healthy brownies made with applesauce instead of oil.
- Sunsweet brand Orange Essence Dried Plums.
- Bowl of assorted healthy nuts such as raw almonds, walnuts, pecans, and cashews.

### Dinner

- Grilled chicken or fish with vegetable-based sauces or salsas.
- Pasta (preferably whole wheat or spinach) with marinara sauce (no cream or pesto) and vegetables.
- Lasagna made with low-fat cheese, vegetables, and marinara sauce.
- Turkey breast with baked sweet potato and steamed or grilled vegetables.
- Entrée salad with grilled chicken or fish and vegetables.
- Whole-grain rolls and bread with olive oil and herbs for dipping.
- Nonfat frozen yogurt and fresh fruit and fat-free sauce.
- Carrot cake made with applesauce instead of oil.

### Movement and Exercise Activities

- At off-site meetings, organize early-morning walks around the facility.
- Schedule several stretch breaks during the day as a supplement to the standard breaks, inviting participants to gently move their arms and legs without leaving their places.

- When the weather permits, have breakout sessions outside where participants walk to a place on the grounds for their discussion.

- Schedule walk-and-talk breakout sessions where small groups of participants continue the discussion as they walk around the building.

- Encourage participants to use the stairs instead of the elevators when they come to and leave the meeting room. Post signs pointing to the stairwells.

- During breaks, play relaxing music and encourage participants to use the time to relax and refresh themselves rather than check their messages.

- Provide prizes that encourage exercise—water bottles, headbands, T-shirts, sweatshirts, and small weights.

A good source of information is American Cancer Society, *Meeting Well: A Tool for Planning Meetings and Events,* Atlanta, Ga.: American Cancer Society, 2000.

**Related Tools**
- Preparing for Your Next Meeting (tool #2)
- Components of a New Team Kick-Off Meeting (tool #8)
- Planning an Off-Site Meeting That's On Target (tool #9)
- Serious Fun at Team Meetings? You're Kidding (tool #24)

# PART 3

# CLOSING AND FOLLOWING UP ON THE MEETING

# 26

# ENDING MEETINGS ON TIME
# AND ON TARGET

## *Purpose*

Closing your meeting in a positive and professional manner takes only a few minutes, yet done well, it can be an effective team-building activity. A solid closing will give members a sense of accomplishment, eliminate any confusion about decisions or agreements, prepare members to clearly communicate with their various stakeholders, and motivate them to take the actions necessary to support the team's goals.

This tool lists the steps to a positive, powerful closing.

## Ending the Meeting: Step by Step

1. *Review the major decisions, agreements, and points covered in the meeting.* You may choose to ask the team scribe to handle this task. A review does two things: it ensures clear communication because members hear the decisions again and have another chance to clarify or edit them, and it ensures the scribe has accurately recorded the decisions and other action items in the notes.

2. *Review the new action items, including the members responsible and the due dates.* As appropriate, you may also review the status of other outstanding action items. This activity serves to remind team members of their commitments. Once again, the scribe can handle this task.

3. *As appropriate, set the date, time, and site of your next team meeting.* If necessary, review other meetings that involve subgroups of the team that will take place between this meeting and the next full team meeting.

4. *Evaluate the effectiveness of the meeting.* See the next three tools for meeting evaluation (two-minute, five-minute, and ten-minute).

5. *Thank the members.* In particular, note those who made special contributions to the success of the meeting by, for example, preparing a document or delivering a presentation. Recognition is free, so spread it around liberally!

**Related Tools**

- Preparing for Your Next Meeting (tool #2)
- How to Prepare an Action Agenda (tool #3)
- Defining Team Meeting Roles (tool #4)
- Meeting Time Management (tool #12)
- Meeting Evaluation: A Two-Minute Drill (tool #27)
- Meeting Evaluation: A Five-Minute Activity (tool #28)
- Meeting Evaluation: A Ten-Minute Assessment (tool #29)
- Meeting Notes (tool #30)
- Getting Action on Action Items (tool #31)

# 27

# MEETING EVALUATION

## *A TWO-MINUTE DRILL*

## *Purpose*

The Two-Minute Meeting Evaluation will enable you to obtain immediate feedback on the effectiveness of your team meeting and identify ways to improve your next meeting. It is designed to be used at the end of every team meeting.

This evaluation takes about two to three minutes to complete. Be sure to set aside a bit of time for it at the end of the meeting agenda. All you will need is some method of recording responses for the group to see—a flip chart, whiteboard, overhead projector, or LCD projector.

### The Process

1. Create two columns on your chart or display screen. Write a plus (+) sign at the top of the left column and the delta (^) sign at the top of the right column.

2. Indicate that the purpose of the exercise is to collect the members' comments on the aspects of today's meeting that went well and should be continued (the + column) and the aspects that should be eliminated or changed (the ^ column).

3. Explain that brainstorming is free-flowing, no-holds-barred, rapid-fire outpouring of ideas without judgment or evaluation. Encourage members to simply throw out ideas.

4. Begin by asking for ideas under both categories. As the ideas come out, write them in the appropriate column.

5. Conclude the session by reviewing the ideas and summarizing any obvious themes such as these:

- "Looks like you like the idea of receiving the agenda a week in advance."

- "It appears that the side conversation during the meeting is very distracting."

6. Assure the team that you will incorporate the ideas as you plan and carry out the next team meeting.

**Related Tools**

- Ending Meetings On Time and On Target (tool #26)
- Meeting Evaluation: A Five-Minute Activity (tool #28)
- Meeting Evaluation: A Ten-Minute Assessment (tool #29)

# 28

# MEETING EVALUATION

## *A FIVE-MINUTE ACTIVITY*

## *Purpose*

The Five-Minute Meeting Evaluation will enable you to collect feedback on the effectiveness of your team meeting and identify ways to improve your next meeting. Since this approach takes a little more time, it is designed to be used on a quarterly basis.

This evaluation takes about five minutes to complete. Be sure to set aside time for it on the meeting agenda.

### The Process

1. Have a copy of the Five-Minute Meeting Evaluation questionnaire for each team member. You can speed the process by distributing it to each member with the meeting agenda. *Note:* Select one of the three variations at the end of this chapter based on the current needs of your team.

2. Explain that the purpose of the exercise is to obtain their feedback on the effectiveness of today's meeting.

3. Ask members to take out their copies of the questionnaire if it was distributed in advance; otherwise hand out copies now.

4. Ask each person to quickly jot down a few notes in response to the questions. Allow sixty seconds for this.

5. Facilitate a discussion beginning with the first question. Allow ninety seconds to two minutes on this question. Ask the meeting scribe to take notes on the discussion, and those that follow.

6. Facilitate a discussion on the second question. Allow two to two and one-half minutes.

7. Conclude with a brief summary of the key ideas for meeting effectiveness, for example:

   - "It looks like you're saying that we need to reduce the number of agenda items so we can focus on the most important issues."

   - "At the next meeting you want me to start the meeting on time no matter how few people are in the room."

8. Collect the questionnaires at the end of the meeting. Prepare a summary for distribution to the team. You may use the summary as the basis for a discussion at a future meeting.

### Five-Minute Meeting Evaluation Questionnaire, Variation 1

1. How do you feel about the way the meeting was planned and carried out?

2. In what ways can our future meetings be improved?

### Five-Minute Meeting Evaluation Questionnaire, Variation 2

1. How do you feel about what was accomplished at today's meeting?

2. What suggestions do you have for our next meeting? Pre-meeting planning? Agenda? Physical/technical arrangements? Meeting facilitation? Other?

### Five-Minute Meeting Evaluation Variation 3

Please complete these sentences.

1. I felt that the meeting . . .

2. At our next meeting, I would like us to . . .

**Related Tools**

- Ending Meetings On Time and On Target (tool #26)
- Meeting Evaluation: A Two-Minute Drill (tool #27)
- Meeting Evaluation: A Ten-Minute Assessment (tool #29)

# 29

# MEETING EVALUATION

## *Purpose*

The Ten-Minute Meeting Evaluation will enable you to obtain detailed feedback on the effectiveness of your team meetings as a prelude to engaging in a self-directed process to improve them.

This evaluation is designed for use on a semiannual or annual basis, at the completion of a significant milestone, or as part of a project review.

This evaluation requires ten minutes to complete the survey and an additional forty-five minutes to one hour to review a summary of the survey data and develop a plan for improvement. Be sure to set aside time on the meeting agenda to complete the survey.

### The Process

1. Give each member a copy of the Ten-Minute Meeting Evaluation questionnaire.

2. Explain the purpose of the exercise. Indicate that you will collect the completed forms and prepare a summary, and that each member of the team will receive a copy of the summary along with the notice and agenda for the next meeting.

3. After the meeting, prepare a summary report that includes a mean for each item and the verbatim comments from the final two questions. Send a copy of the report to each team member along with the meeting notice and agenda for the next team meeting.

4. At the next meeting, begin by outlining the action planning process as follows:

- Provide a brief opportunity for everyone to review the summary and ask questions for clarification of the results.

- Identify the strengths of your meetings by highlighting items with a mean of 3.0 or higher. Facilitate a brief discussion of the positive actions in each of the strength areas.

- Identify the areas of needed improvement by highlighting items with a mean less than 3.0, with special emphasis on items with a mean less than 2.5. Facilitate a discussion focusing on the causes of the low ratings and what needs to change.

- If time permits, divide the team into subgroups and ask each subgroup to develop an action plan for one of the improvement areas and report back at this meeting or the next one. Otherwise, create the subgroups and ask them to work off-line and report their plans at the next team meeting.

## Ten-Minute Meeting Evaluation Questionnaire

Please think about your team's most recent meetings. Assess the extent to which the statements in the following questionnaire are true, using this scale:

4. Almost Always: 81–100 percent of the time

3. Most of the Time: 61–80 percent of the time

2. Occasionally: 31–60 percent of the time

1. Rarely: 0–30 percent of the time

| Statements | Please circle one number |
|---|---|
| 1. Our team meetings have a detailed agenda. | 1    2    3    4 |
| 2. Members receive the agenda and related documents at least three days prior to the meeting. | 1    2    3    4 |

| **Statements** | **Please circle one number** |
|---|---|
| 3. Our meetings start on time. | 1   2   3   4 |
| 4. We make effective use of meeting technology. | 1   2   3   4 |
| 5. We apply an established set of ground rules. | 1   2   3   4 |
| 6. As appropriate, we follow the meeting agenda. | 1   2   3   4 |
| 7. When required, we arrive at a decision in a timely manner. | 1   2   3   4 |
| 8. Communication among members from different sites and cultures is effective. | 1   2   3   4 |
| 9. Key decisions and action items are summarized before the meeting concludes. | 1   2   3   4 |
| 10. Our meetings end on time. | 1   2   3   4 |

*Comments (Please be specific):*

A. What aspects of your team meetings are effective?

B. What recommendations do you have for improving your team meetings?

## Related Tools

- Ending Meetings On Time and On Target (tool #26)
- Meeting Evaluation: A Two-Minute Drill (tool #27)
- Meeting Evaluation: A Five-Minute Activity (tool #28)

# 30

# MEETING NOTES

## CAPTURING THE ESSENCE OF YOUR MEETING

## *Purpose*

Meeting notes differ from meeting minutes. While minutes include a detailed report on everything that took place during the meeting, notes present a summary of the key meeting outcomes and action items.

The purpose of meeting notes is to give a clear but brief synopsis of the meeting's highlights. Members, stakeholders, and others seeking more detailed information on the team's decisions, including documentation, should be able to easily access it at the Team Space or via attachments.

### A Template for Meeting Notes

- Date, time, and location of the meeting.

- Names of members and guests present. Some teams also record the names of members absent.

- List of key outcomes and decisions. It is especially important to capture key words or phrases that will prompt attendees' memory of the topic.

- Action items: New, completed, and outstanding.

- Next meeting date, time, and location.

- Links to or attachments of relevant documents.

Shortly after the meeting, the notes should be prepared by the scribe and reviewed by the team leader or facilitator. Every effort should be made to transmit the notes to the members quickly. In their ground rules some teams establish a specific time requirement for communicating the notes to members (for example, "within five days after the meeting").

Some organizations already have a required template for meeting notes. If your organization has one, of course you need to use it—but if not, consider using the one that follows, which incorporates the essential items.

---

## BLANDER PROJECT TEAM MEETING

**MEETING NOTES**

December 3, 2006

Members Present: A. Bergen, C. Davia, E. Finn, G. Hockner, I. Johari, K. Logano, M. Nadler, O. Parker.

Members Absent: A. Betancourt, C. Davenport.

Key Decisions and Outcomes:

1. The team agreed on an action plan to address the impurities and degradation products in the tablet.

| What | Who | When |
|---|---|---|
| (1) Determine the extent of the problem | A. Bergen | 01/15/07 |
| (2) Meet with field representatives | C. Davia | 01/22/07 |
| (3) Summarize data from the focus groups | E. Finn | 01/25/07 |
| (4) Prepare a report with detailed recommendations | G. Hockner | 02/15/07 |

2. The team accepted Klaus's proposal for addressing the recommendations of the Blander Task Force. A copy of the proposal and plan is on the Blander Team Space.

3. The team approved the Blander Marketing plan. A copy of the plan is on the Team Space.

4. While attending the APRT meeting next week, Edward and Gerhard will meet with Qualicon to explore a possible joint project to study possible contraindications. They will report to the team at the next team meeting.

5. The team expressed its dissatisfaction with the level of detail in the reports from Sigma. By January 12 Andrew will send a letter to Sigma outlining the reporting requirements in the contract.

6. The key milestone chart is being reviewed by senior management in preparation for a full team discussion at the January 15 meeting. Please send your comments and questions to Marshall by January 12.

7. Action Items

| Action | What | Who | When (or Status) |
| --- | --- | --- | --- |
| Relationship with Marketing Consultant | Prepare a list of options and recommendations | AB, CD, EF | Completed 12/21 |
| Marketing Plan Revisions | Make corrections and additions and submit final draft | GH with input from all team members | January 31 |
| Blander Project Expansion | Prepare and submit proposal | KL | Completed 12/31 |
| Blander Sales Plan | Prepare plan | AB | Approved 12/31 |
| Possible joint project with Qualicon | Meet with Qualicon people at APRT | EF & GH | January 15 |

8. Next Meeting: January 15, 2007, 8:30–10:00 A.M., Madison Room 203.

## Related Tools

- How to Prepare an Action Agenda (tool #3)
- Defining Team Meeting Roles (tool #4)
- Getting Action on Action Items (tool #31)

# 31

# GETTING ACTION ON ACTION ITEMS

## *Purpose*

It's easy to focus so much on what happens during the meeting that you forget that the success of a team is equally predicated upon actions outside the meeting (things like agenda planning and follow-up). The work done by members between meetings is critical to moving a project forward, making the best decision, solving an important problem, or developing a detailed plan. This ongoing work often involves the identification and completion of action items that arise during meetings.

Perhaps more important, the successful completion of action items contributes to the development of team trust and a general esprit de corps among members. As members see that they can rely on their teammates to deliver on their commitments, the group takes a giant leap in the direction of becoming a high-performing team.

As a result, getting action on action items is an important factor in both project success and team development. The purpose of this tool is to provide proven tips for facilitating the timely completion of action items.

**Tips for Getting Action on Action Items**

- Make sure that every action item write-up indicates the action required, the due date, and the person responsible.

- Restate the details of the action item as it comes up during the meeting.

- Where possible, write the details on a flip chart or screen.

- At the end of the meeting, review the list of new and continuing action items.

- As appropriate, mention how the action item contributes to the project goals.

- List the action items in the meeting notes. See tool #30, "Meeting Notes."

- Include the action items due at the meeting in the meeting notice and agenda. See tool #3, "How to Prepare an Action Agenda."

- For critical action items, call the responsible person before the due date to ask about the item and see if the person needs help.

- Ensure that your team's ground rules cover behaviors governing the responsibilities of members regarding action items. For example:

    ◆ Inform the team leader when I am unable to attend a meeting (or complete an action item) as soon as I know.

    ◆ Provide the team leader with my completed action items prior to the meeting if I am unable to attend the meeting.

    See tool #7, "Establishing Your Team's Ground Rules."

- If a member does not deliver on a critical action item (and does not inform you in advance), speak directly (not via e-mail) to the person. State the agreement as you understand it and ask when the person expects to complete the work. Ask if the person needs help. At the conclusion of the conversation, ask for a new agreement on the task. Finally, ask to be notified if the new deadline looks like it is slipping. You can say something along these lines:

    "Danielle, it was my understanding that you agreed to provide the new data from the site by March 12. Is that correct? Since, as you know, these data are critical, can you tell me when we will have your report? I realize that you are very busy right now, so please tell me if you need some help in getting this work done. OK, so you're saying that we will have the data by the end of this month. Danielle, that will be fine, but please let me know as soon as possible if you are unable to get the work done by then."

- The meeting notes should include a table that presents the status of the team's action items. Here is an example of such a table:

| Action | What | Who | When (or Status) |
| --- | --- | --- | --- |
| Sales Development Plan | Complete plan | Danielle, Jack, & Juan | December 12 |
| Marketing Plan Revisions | Incorporate revisions and submit final draft to management team | Gabriella, with input from all team members | January 31 |
| Team Building Off-Site Meeting | Develop agenda with BH | David & Pat | Completed December 31 |
| Training Proposal | Review proposal and meet with GP | Alexandra | Approved December 31 |
| Possible joint project with Qualicon | Meet with Qualicon people at APRT | EF & GH | January 15 |

## Related Tools

- How to Prepare an Action Agenda (tool #3)
- Establishing Your Team's Ground Rules (tool #7)
- Ending Meetings On Time and On Target (tool #26)
- Meeting Notes (tool #30)
- After-Meeting Actions (tool #32)
- Managing External Communications (tool #33)

# 32

# AFTER-MEETING ACTIONS

## *Purpose*

Just as pre-meeting planning and preparation helps ensure a successful meeting, post-meeting action also contributes to an effective meeting outcome. The after-meeting action begins with a thoughtful meeting closing that includes a summary of key decisions, a review of action items, and an evaluation of the meeting process (see tool #25, "Ending Meetings On Time and On Target").

While busy schedules may encourage the tendency to do little until planning begins for the next meeting, it is important to see follow-up as part of the total meeting process. As a result, we suggest that both the facilitator and the members invest some time in actions designed to carry the meeting forward into the future. In this area, a small amount of considered effort can have a big impact on meeting and team effectiveness.

The purpose of this tool is to provide a few key tips for the meeting facilitator as well as for the team members.

### Tips for the Meeting Facilitator

- In conjunction with the meeting scribe, review the notes and transmit them to the team and key stakeholders as soon as possible. (See tool #30, "Meeting Notes.")

- Talk with key stakeholders about relevant issues that were discussed or decided at the meeting.

- Contact team members who are responsible for critical action items. Offer to provide help, resources, or other support. Ask that they inform you if they have difficulty completing the assignment.

- Meet with team members who appear to have issues or concerns about the team or the meeting. For example, those who seem unhappy with a team decision, those who have conflicts with other members, and anyone who rarely participates in discussions, consistently arrives late or leaves early, or multi-tasks during the meeting. (See tool # 23, "Managing Meeting Monsters.")

- Honor your commitments to members and others. Nothing increases your credibility more with both members and stakeholders than serving as a role model of responsible after-meeting behavior.

- Quickly implement all decisions agreed to at the meeting.

- Review the end-of-meeting evaluation to identify any actions you can implement at the next meeting. (See tools #27– #29, the two-minute, five-minute, and ten-minute meeting evaluations.)

- Take a few minutes to reflect on your performance as meeting facilitator. What did you do well? What could be improved? What will you do differently at the next meeting?

### Tips for the Meeting Participant

- Quickly begin working on your action items. Do not wait until you receive the notes. *Note:* Be sure to clarify the team's expectations about your action items before you leave the meeting or shortly thereafter.

- If decisions were made or issues raised during the meeting that concern your area, have a review meeting or conversation with your manager as soon as possible.

- Offer to plan, facilitate, or prepare materials for any relevant subgroup meetings scheduled to be held after the team meeting.

- Provide feedback to the team leader and meeting facilitator about meeting process or any other issues that you think are relevant to team success.

- Where possible, if other team members seem to be overloaded with work and have responsibility for important team action items, offer to help.

### Be Alert to the After-Meeting "Meeting"

At times, you may notice a small group of team members holding an informal (usually unplanned) gathering after the meeting in the hallway, cafeteria, or office. Sometimes these get-togethers are simply task groups trying to divide the work or follow up on something discussed or decided at the meeting.

However, in other cases, these are complaint sessions where members voice their dissatisfaction with such things as lack of progress, poor meeting practices, ineffective leadership, or work stress. It is possible that these members do not feel comfortable raising their concerns in an open meeting. If members do not feel the meeting climate supports open communication, this is a serious matter. Therefore, when you become aware of these "meetings," quick action is required. Your goal should be to first understand the complaints and then put the issues on the formal meeting agenda as soon as possible.

### Related Tools

- Managing Meeting Monsters (tool #23)
- Ending Meetings On Time and On Target (tool #26)
- Meeting Evaluation: A Two-Minute Drill (tool #27)
- Meeting Evaluation: A Five-Minute Activity (tool #28)
- Meeting Evaluation: A Ten-Minute Assessment (tool #29)
- Meeting Notes (tool #30)

# 33

# MANAGING EXTERNAL COMMUNICATIONS

## *Purpose*

Team success—and meeting excellence—is greatly influenced (some might even say controlled) by people outside the team. Senior management, functional managers, subject matter experts, support groups, government regulators, and vendors and suppliers all may play a role in the success of a team. As a result, communication with these stakeholders about meeting outcomes is critical to team success.

The key to communication about team issues addressed in a meeting is to determine what to communicate, to whom, when, and in what format. Many teams take this issue for granted, assuming that it is sufficient to send out their meeting notes to a long list of e-mail recipients.

A useful team exercise is to spend a few minutes thinking about why external communication is important for team success. The outcome of such an exercise usually finds the following listed as reasons to communicate with external stakeholders:

Obtain new support, including resources, for your project.

Maintain existing support for your project.

Eliminate obstacles faced by your team or project.

Solicit ideas, feedback, and expertise on team issues or problems.

Reduce external interference with your project.

Inform and educate about the work of your team.

The communication issues faced by a team require answers to the following questions:

- What should be communicated?
- To whom should it be communicated?
- When should it be communicated?
- Why should it be communicated?
- How should it be communicated?

That last point is worth considering in some detail. Sometimes, as Marshall McLuhan said, the medium is the message—or at any rate it conveys a message of its own. It is fair to conclude that a team should carefully consider the best way to communicate with its stakeholders because the method may have a considerable impact on the effectiveness of the outcome. For example, simply forwarding a major change in your project plan as an e-mail attachment may fail to convince your management sponsor, whereas a face-to-face or telephone conversation where you can provide a detailed explanation and answer questions may be more effective in obtaining the approval you seek.

The purpose of this tool is to provide tips for answering the five key questions of communication.

## What Should Be Communicated?

- *Meeting notes.* This document, which contains the decisions and action items of meeting, is the principal vehicle of external team communication. While it is easy take the content of the document for granted, your team should spend time thinking about the answers to these questions:
    - Why do we want this person to read the notes?
    - Has this person asked to be on the distribution list?

- Have you ever received any comments on the notes from this person?

- Does this person need all the attachments, such as the presentation slides and reports?

- *Project plans.* This document, which sets the direction and defines the objectives of the team, is an important team product. A key question for the team is to decide which stakeholders only need to see an executive summary of the plan, and which need the whole thing. Consider the following stakeholders:

  - Those who approve the plan

  - Those who provide resources that support the plan

  - Those who help implement the plan

- *Progress reports.* Monthly, quarterly, or annual reports are often seen by a wider audience than the more detailed documents such as meeting notes and project plans. For your team it is important to determine who sees these documents.

- *Problems and obstacles.* A document that describes a problem, obstacle, or barrier faced by the team is generally seen by a narrow audience. Typically, team problems are directed to the stakeholder who can help provide a solution or remove the obstacle.

- *Success stories.* As your team accomplishes a goal, achieves a successful outcome, or receives some favorable feedback, it is appropriate to communicate your success to a wide range of stakeholders.

- *Resource requests.* At times your team will need a budget increase, additional expertise, or other technical resources. The rationale for such a request should be as well considered as the submission process and the list of persons receiving the request.

**To Whom Should the Team Communicate?**

It is important for the team to decide which stakeholders should receive each type of communication. These are the typical recipients of team communications:

- Senior management
- Team sponsor (sometimes a senior manager)
- Functional department manager (function is represented on the team)
- Core team members
- Ad hoc team members
- Support groups
- Vendors and suppliers
- Regulatory agencies

**When Should the Team Communicate?**

- The frequency of communication is often determined by the recipient. The team sponsor may want to see all team outputs as they become available, while senior management may only need to see the quarterly progress report.
- The frequency of the communication is also determined by the nature of the document. For example, the meeting notes are sent as soon as possible after the meeting, while the regular progress report might be distributed monthly.
- Problems need to be communicated immediately.
- Intrateam communications are usually sent
  - Immediately or as required
  - Immediately after each meeting
  - Monthly

* Quarterly
* Annually

## Why Should the Team Communicate?

* *Seek approval.* Some proposals or decisions require the approval of a key stakeholder or several stakeholders with decision-making authority. A budget proposal, for example, almost always requires approval by a member of management.

* *Inform.* Some team actions or documents are sent to stakeholders with the goal of keeping them up to date about the work of the team.

* *Consult.* Teams will often be required to give some stakeholders an opportunity to offer an opinion on a proposed action or conclusion.

* *Seek expert advice.* Sometimes a team will voluntarily ask technical or scientific experts to review a proposed action or document and provide the benefit of their expertise.

## How Should the Team Communicate?

* *Face-to-face meeting.* A personal meeting with a key stakeholder has all the advantages of two-way communication, informal interaction, and the opportunity to read nonverbal cues that make this method ideal for seeking approval, soliciting opinion, and obtaining expert input. However, given the difficulty and sometimes the expense of scheduling an in-person meeting, this method should be reserved for important team issues.

* *Staff and management meeting.* Some communications are best handled at a group meeting where you present the information to your colleagues or management team. In some situations, this is the required method. Use of this approach gives you the opportunity to get feedback from a number of people and hear the issues debated in an open forum where you can participate. However, remember that

this method requires excellent presentation, verbal communication, and group interaction skills on the part of the person representing the team.

- *Via a sponsor.* If your team has a senior management sponsor (and we recommend it for most teams), this person is often best positioned to be the team's spokesperson and advocate for additional resources, approval of a project plan, elimination of organizational barriers, or other key decisions. One disadvantage is the tendency to overuse or rely solely on your sponsor to the exclusion of other methods.

- *E-mail.* Electronic mail has the advantages of speed, 24/7 communication, and the opportunity to provide a great deal of detail. It is often the best way to communicate with stakeholders who are located around the world. The disadvantages include all the barriers associated with one-way communication:

  - No same-time feedback

  - No opportunity to read nonverbal reactions

  - Possibility of misunderstanding the meaning of some words

  - Little opportunity to express emotion

- *Telephone.* If you are able to have a telephone conversation with a stakeholder, this is the next best method to a face-to-face meeting. It offers you many of the advantages of two-way communication, and is therefore recommended for important issues such as problems and obstacles and resource requests. Disadvantages include the obvious ones such as inability to gauge nonverbal reactions and the difficulty of scheduling a telephone conversation with stakeholders in widely different time zones.

- *Ad hoc.* Sometimes the most effective approach is the unplanned, informal conversation that takes place in a hallway, the cafeteria, or just before or after a meeting. The one caution about the use of this method is the need to be prepared and, therefore, ready to have a productive meeting when the opportunity presents itself. Some teams have been known to "plan" an ad hoc meeting by positioning one of their members in a spot where a key stakeholder is likely to pass by.

## TEAM EXERCISE

Many teams find that the completion of this table at a meeting is a useful exercise. While you may need to edit the "What" column to tailor the table to the needs of your team, simply going through the process of completing the table will help ensure that your external communication is successful.

| WHAT | TO WHOM | WHEN* | WHY** | HOW*** |
|---|---|---|---|---|
| Meeting Notes | | | | |
| Project Plan | | | | |
| Successes | | | | |
| Problems | | | | |
| Resources | | | | |
| Progress | | | | |

Note: The following codes will simplify completion of each column:

* P = Post-meeting; M = Monthly; Q = Quarterly; A = Annual; AR = As required

** I = Inform; A = Seek approval; C = Consult (seek opinion); E = Seek expertise

*** F2F = Face-to-face; EM = E-mail; P = Phone; M = Meeting (staff); AH = Ad hoc; S = Sponsor

**Related Tools**

- Defining Team Meeting Roles (tool #4)
- E-Mail Excellence (tool #11)
- Meeting Notes (tool #30)
- After-Meeting Actions (tool #32)

PART 4

RESOURCES

## WEB-BASED MEETING TOOLS

### *Purpose*

As global teams and other geographically dispersed teams increase in both number and importance and the cost of travel grows, the need for effective alternatives to face-to-face meetings correspondingly increases. The two most popular alternatives are videoconferencing and teleconferencing.

Videoconferences are popular because meeting participants can see as well as hear their teammates. However, the technology is expensive, subject to breakdowns, and requires some technical expertise to manage. Teleconferencing is still more popular because it is inexpensive, easy to operate, rarely breaks down, and allows team members to call in from multiple locations. However, facilitating the meeting is more difficult because of the lack of visual support.

The Internet provides some useful alternatives in the form of supports for facilitating meetings of so-called virtual teams. Our purpose here is to present some of these Web-based meeting tools. However, a caution is in order. As we have observed over the years, tools of this type have a limited life. Software comes on the market, is heavily promoted for a period of time, but soon disappears if sales are not strong. Therefore, we cannot guarantee that the tools reviewed here will still be available by the time you read this. On the other hand, some new and perhaps better tools may have been developed in the interim. Look for features that match or surpass the ones that appeal to you from these discussions.

### Tools for Virtual Team Meetings

- *Microsoft Live Meeting.* With a PC, a phone, and an Internet connection, you are ready to use Live Meeting to set up your team meeting, invite participants, display PowerPoint slides, brainstorm using a whiteboard, poll the participants for a decision, and get instant feedback from participants. No special software is required and it can be used from any Microsoft application. Mac users can also use the system. For a quick look or a more elaborate 30-minute demo, go to http://main.livemeeting.com.

- *Centra.* The Centra service is especially useful for real-time document review and markup by a team. It's great for a multiregion sales team pulling together a proposal for a national account or a project team creating a statement of work. Centra allows you to take care of the basics such as scheduling the meeting, identifying the number of participants, including video, and allowing users to join without an invitation or join during a meeting. You choose between Voice over Internet or telephone communication mode. During the meeting participants can chat with each other, mark up a document, ask other people with specific expertise to join the meeting, get the sense of the group with a quick poll, and easily share other files. You can also record the meeting for future reference and playback. For more information and to participate in a demo, log on to www.centra.com.

- *Tanberg.* This company provides a wireless videoconferencing system that runs on a LAN. As a result, if you want to have the benefit of video at your next team meeting, the location is not restricted to just the few rooms in the building with video capability. The minimum required components at each location are a microphone, a camera, a codec, a monitor, and a speaker. The camera and microphone capture the image and sound; the codec converts the video and audio into a digital signal, encodes it, and sends it out. The codec at the other end decodes the signal and distributes the video and audio to the monitor and speaker. For more information, check it out at www.tandberg.net.

- *eRoom.* Although this system does not support video or audio, it allows a team to store all materials related to the project—all the documents, e-mail messages, action items, and discussions, as well as all the meeting notes. It includes tools to assist with group edits, whiteboard sessions, real-time discussions, and one-to-many presentations.

With this tool, distributed teams can work simultaneously on project documents and can capture, index, and reuse the collective output of a session. You can also incorporate and share files and folders from your hard drive using the system's drag-and-drop feature. And, of course, there is no reason why you can't add audio via a teleconference so you can talk about the editing of a document or preparation of a presentation. After you register at www.eroom.net, you can experience a demo of the system in action.

- *Hot Office.* This service allows you to hold online team conferences, upload documents to a secure file or folder, control access to those documents, view presentations and other documents without downloading, edit documents (and control who can edit them), set up private chats, and take care of many other useful team meeting tasks without the time and cost of a face-to-face meeting. For more information, go to www.hotoffice.com.

- *WebEx.* One of the older, more established services, WebEx has a good site that allows you to experience a useful short demo that explains and demonstrates their virtual meeting features. Using multiple windows, you can simultaneously see a list of the current meeting participants, study a slide, and view a video. You can annotate and highlight a slide and make changes to documents on the fly. The meeting facilitator can also hand over meeting leadership to another participant, chat with one or all of the meeting attendees, and bring up a whiteboard for brainstorming or to record a discussion. Team members can call in to the meeting or receive a call back if they cannot locate the number. As with other similar services, you can choose to use either a telephone line or Voice over Internet for communication as well as record your meeting for playback at a later time and by others not at the meeting. With an additional download you can set up a quick meeting with their one-click meeting option. To access the demo and other information, log on to www.webex.com.

**Related Tools**

- Communicating in a Videoconference (tool #16)
- Teleconference Tips (tool #17)
- Presenting at a Team Meeting (tool #20)

# THE SEVEN SINS OF DEADLY MEETINGS

*And seven steps to salvation.* Tools, techniques, and technologies to make your meetings less painful, more productive—even heavenly.

Naomi Chavez, an internal consultant for Cisco Systems, one of Silicon Valley's leading network-equipment manufacturers, is frustrated: "We have the most ineffective meetings of any company I've ever seen."

Kevin Eassa, vice president of operations for the disk division of Conner Peripherals, another Silicon Valley giant, is realistically resigned: "We realize our meetings are unproductive. A consulting firm is trying to help us, and we think they've hit the mark. But we've got a long way to go."

Richard Collard, senior manager of network operations at Federal Express, is simply exasperated: "We just seem to meet and meet and meet and we never seem to do anything."

Meetings are the most universal—and universally despised—part of business life. But bad meetings do more than ruin an otherwise pleasant day. William R. Daniels, senior consultant at American Consulting & Training of Mill Valley, California, has introduced meeting-improvement techniques to companies including Applied Materials and Motorola. He is adamant about the real stakes: bad meetings make bad companies.

"Meetings matter because that's where an organization's culture perpetuates itself," he says. "Meetings are how an organization says, 'You are a member.' So if every day we go to boring meetings full of boring people, then we can't help but think that this is a boring company. Bad meetings are a source of negative messages about our company and ourselves."

---

*Note:* By Eric Matson, © 2005 Graner + Jahr USA Publishing. First published in *Fast Company*, April-May 1996, p. 122. Reprinted with permission.

It's not supposed to be this way. In a business world that is faster, tougher, leaner, and more downsized than ever, you might expect the sheer demands of competition (not to mention the impact of e-mail and groupware) to curb our appetite for meetings. In reality, the opposite may be true. As more work becomes teamwork, and fewer people remain to do the work that exists, the number of meetings is likely to increase rather than decrease. Jon Ryburg, president of the Facility Performance Group in Ann Arbor, Michigan, is an organizational psychologist who advises companies on office design and "meeting ergonomics." He tells his clients that they need twice as much meeting space as they did 20 years ago. The reason? "More and more companies are team-based companies, and in team-based companies most work gets done in meetings."

A variety of tools and techniques (plus a healthy dose of common sense) can make meetings less painful, more productive, maybe even fun. There's also an important role for technology, although the undeniable power of computer-enabled meeting systems usually comes with astronomical price tags. Still, there's lots to learn from electronic "meetingware" even if you never buy it. What follows is *Fast Company*'s guide to the seven sins of deadly meetings and, more important, seven steps to salvation.

*Sin #1: People don't take meetings seriously.* They arrive late, leave early, and spend most of their time doodling.
*Salvation:* Adopt Intel's mind-set that meetings are real work.

There are as many techniques to improve the "crispness" of meetings as there are items on the typical meeting agenda. Some companies punish latecomers with a penalty fee or reprimand them in the minutes of the meeting. But these techniques address symptoms, not the disease. Disciplined meetings are about mind-set—a shared conviction among all the participants that meetings are real work. That all-too-frequent expression of relief—"Meeting's over, let's get back to work"—is the mortal enemy of good meetings.

"Most people simply don't view going to meetings as doing work," says William Daniels. "You have to make your meetings uptime rather than downtime."

Is there a company with the right mind-set? Daniels nominates Intel, the semiconductor manufacturer famous for its managerial toughness and crisp execution. Walk into any conference room at any Intel factory or office anywhere in the world and you will see on the wall a poster with a series of simple questions about the meetings that take place there. Do you know the purpose of this meeting? Do you have an agenda? Do you know your role? Do you follow the rules for good minutes?

These posters are a visual reminder of just how serious Intel is about productive meetings. Indeed, every new employee, from the most junior production worker to the highest ranking executive, is required to take the company's home-grown course on effective meetings. For years the course was taught by CEO Andy Grove himself, who believed that good meetings were such an important part of Intel's culture that it was worth his time to train the troops. "We talk a lot about meeting discipline," says Michael Fors, corporate training manager at Intel University. "It isn't complicated. It's doing the basics well: structured agendas, clear goals, paths that you're going to follow. These things make a huge difference."

*Sin #2: Meetings are too long.* They should accomplish twice as much in half the time.

*Salvation:* Time is money. Track the cost of your meetings and use computer-enabled simultaneity to make them more productive.

Almost every guru invokes the same rule: meetings should last no longer than 90 minutes. When's the last time your company held to that rule?

One reason meetings drag on is that people don't appreciate how expensive they are. James B. Rieley, director of the Center for Continuous Quality Improvement at the Milwaukee Area Technical College, recently decided to change all that. He did a survey of the college's 130-person management council to find out how much time its members spent in meetings. When he multiplied their time by their salaries, he determined that the college was spending $3 million per year on management-council meetings alone. Money talks: after Rieley's study came out, the college trained 40 people as facilitators to keep meetings on track. Bernard DeKoven, founder of the Institute for Better Meetings in Palo Alto, California, has gone Rieley one step better. He's developed software called the Meeting Meter that allows any team or department to calculate, on a running basis, how much their meetings cost. After someone inputs the names and salaries of meeting participants, the program starts ticking. Think of it as a national debt clock for meetings.

DeKoven emphasizes that he created the Meeting Meter as a conversation piece rather than as a serious management tool. It's a visible way to put meeting productivity on the agenda. "When I use the meter, I don't just talk about the cost of meetings," he says, "I talk about the cost of bad meetings. Because bad meetings lead to even more meetings, and over time the costs become awe-inspiring."

Technology can do more than just keep meetings shorter. It can also increase productivity—that is, help generate more ideas and decisions per minute. One of the main benefits of meetingware is that it allows participants to violate the first rule of good behavior in most other circumstances: wait your turn to speak. With Ventana's GroupSystems V, the most powerful meeting software available today, participants enter their comments and ideas into workstations. The workstations organize the comments and project them onto a monitor for the whole group to see. Most everyone who has studied or participated in computer-enabled meetings agrees that this capacity for simultaneity produces dramatic gains in the number of ideas and the speed with which they are generated.

Geoff Bywater, senior vice president of marketing and promotion for Fox Music, recently organized a strategic retreat for the 170 top executives of 20th Century Fox Filmed Entertainment. He used a computer system supplied by CoVision, a San Francisco consulting firm that specializes in technology-enabled meetings. Apple PowerBooks outfitted with customized software allowed participants to respond to questions, propose ideas, and vote on options—all at the same time.

"We had 170 of the brightest people in the company in one room," Bywater reports. "The challenge was, how much information and how many ideas could we get out of them? Even if we had divided into 15 breakout groups, we'd still have only 15 people speaking at the same time. People were amazed. If we asked a question and each person typed in 2 ideas, that's nearly 350 ideas in five minutes! That was the biggest impact of the technology—the number of ideas generated in such a short time."

Be warned, though: electronic meetings can be more productive than traditional meetings, but they're not always shorter. "The good news about computer-supported meetings is that the discussions tend not to be repetitive or redundant," says Michael Schrage, a consultant on collaborative technologies and the author of *No More Teams,* an influential guide to group work and meetings. "The bad news is that the meetings can become longer. The computer-supported environment encourages people to discuss things a little more thoroughly than they might otherwise."

*Sin #3: People wander off the topic.* Participants spend more time digressing than discussing.

*Salvation:* Get serious about agendas and store distractions in a "parking lot."

It's the starting point for all advice on productive meetings: stick to the agenda. But it's hard to stick to an agenda that doesn't exist, and most meetings in most companies are decidedly agenda-free. "In the real world," says Schrage, "agendas are about as rare as the white rhino. If they do exist, they're about as useful. Who hasn't been in meetings where someone tries to prove that the agenda isn't appropriate?"

Agendas are worth taking seriously. Intel is fanatical about them; it has developed an agenda "template" that everyone in the company uses. Much of the template is unsurprising. An Intel agenda (circulated several days before a meeting to let participants react to and modify it) lists the meeting's key topics, who will lead which parts of the discussion, how long each segment will take, what the expected outcomes are, and so on.

Intel agendas also specify the meeting's decision-making style. The company distinguishes among four approaches to decisions: authoritative (the leader has full responsibility); consultative (the leader makes a decision after weighing group input); voting; and consensus. Being clear and up-front about decision styles, Intel believes, sets the right expectations and helps focus the conversation.

"Going into the meeting, people know how they're giving input and how that input will get rolled up into a decision," says Intel's Michael Fors. "If you don't have structured agendas, and people aren't sure of the decision path, they'll bring up side issues that are related but not directly relevant to solving the problem."

Of course, even the best-crafted agendas can't guard against digressions, distractions, and the other foibles of human interaction. The challenge is to keep meetings focused without stifling creativity or insulting participants who stray. At Ameritech, the regional telephone company based in Chicago, meeting leaders use a "parking lot" to maintain that focus.

"When comments come up that aren't related to the issue at hand, we record them on a flip chart labeled the parking lot," says Kimberly Thomas, director of communications for small business services. But the parking lot isn't a black hole. "We always track the issue and the person responsible for it," she adds. "We use this technique throughout the company."

*Sin #4: Nothing happens once the meeting ends.* People don't convert decisions into action.
*Salvation:* Convert from "meeting" to "doing" and focus on common documents.

The problem isn't that people are lazy or irresponsible. It's that people leave meetings with different views of what happened and what's supposed to happen next. Meeting experts are unanimous on this point: even with the ubiquitous tools of organization and sharing ideas—whiteboards, flip charts, Post-it notes—the capacity for misunderstanding is unlimited. Which is another reason companies turn to computer technology.

The best way to avoid that misunderstanding is to convert from "meeting" to "doing"—where the "doing" focuses on the creation of shared documents that lead to action. The fact is, the most powerful role for technology is also the simplest: recording comments, outlining ideas, generating written proposals, projecting them for the entire group to see, printing them so people leave with real-time minutes. Forget groupware; just get yourself a good outlining program and oversized monitor.

"You're not just having a meeting, you're creating a document," says Michael Schrage. "I can't emphasize enough the importance of that distinction. It is the fundamental difference between ordinary meetings and computer-augmented collaborations. Comments, questions, criticisms, insights should enhance the quality of the document. That should be the group's mission."

In other words, the medium is the meeting. That's why Bernard DeKoven prefers computers to flip charts and whiteboards. "Flip charts create behaviors conditioned by the medium," he says. "People start competing for room on the flip chart, the facilitator has to scratch things out, and pretty soon you can't read what's on it. With a computer, you never run out of room for ideas, you can edit indefinitely, you can generate hard copies for everyone at a moment's notice. It's a much richer medium."

*Sin #5: People don't tell the truth.* There's plenty of conversation, but not much candor.
*Salvation:* Embrace anonymity.

We all know it's true: Too often, people in meetings simply don't speak their minds. Sometimes the problem is a leader who doesn't solicit participation. Sometimes a dominant personality intimidates the rest of the group. But most of the time the problem is a simple lack of trust. People don't feel secure enough to say what they really think.

The most powerful techniques to promote candor rely on technology, and most of these computer-based tools focus on anonymity—enabling people to express opinions and evaluate alternatives without having to divulge their identities. It's a sobering commentary on free speech in business—"Say what you think, and we'll disguise your names to protect the innocent"—but it does seem to work.

Jay Nunamaker, CEO of Ventana Corporation, based in Tucson, Arizona, and a professor at the University of Arizona's Karl Eller Graduate School of Management, is a leading expert on electronic meetings. He says Ventana added anonymity to its software to meet the needs of the U.S. military. "Admirals can really dampen interaction at a meeting," he notes. "But we didn't realize the impact it would have in corporate settings. Even with people who work together all the time, anonymity changes the social protocols. People say things differently." CoVision, the firm that facilitated the 20th Century Fox meeting, provides a system that allows for anonymous voting and anonymous group conversations. Meeting participants enter comments onto laptops, and the comments are projected onto a screen without attribution. CoVision president Lenny Lind says the system is especially powerful in meetings of high-ranking executives.

"People in the upper reaches of management pay so much deference to the leader, and have so much to lose, that conversations quickly become measured and political," he argues. "People just won't bare their souls. Anonymity changes that."

But there are problems with anonymity. Some people like getting credit for their ideas, and anonymity can leave them feeling shortchanged. There are also opportunities for manipulation. Carol Anne Ogdin of Deep Woods Technology, a teamwork consultant and meeting facilitator based in Santa Clara, California, calls anonymity a "modest idea that's been blown out of proportion." In particular, she worries about gamesmanship—for example, people who build an anonymous groundswell of support for their own contributions.

*Sin #6: Meetings are always missing important information, so they postpone critical decisions.*
*Salvation:* Get data, not just furniture, into meeting rooms.

Most meeting rooms make it harder to have good meetings. They're sterile and uninviting—and often in the middle of nowhere. Why? To help people "concentrate" by removing them from the frenzy of office life. But this isolation leaves meeting rooms out of the information flow. Often, the downside of isolation outweighs the benefits of focus.

Computer-services giant EDS has built a set of high-tech facilities that leave meeting participants awash in data. These much-heralded Capture Labs, electronic meeting rooms used by the company and its clients, may offer a glimpse of the meeting room of the future.

The Capture Lab "is a self-contained information network," says Michael Bauer, a principal with EDS's management consulting subsidiary. "We can bring in information from the Internet or from EDS's internal Web. We can get information on stock prices, even about the weather if we're worried about shipping or travel. It's brought into the room, displayed on a screen, and talked about."

It's not necessary to go that far. Jon Ryburg, the meeting ergonomist, offers a few ways to increase the "information quotient" in meeting spaces. For one thing, allow enough space in your meeting rooms for teams to store materials. Project teams generate lots more than minutes and memos. Meetings build models, fill up flip charts, create artifacts of all sorts—"information" that's vital to future meetings. "People are constantly hauling materials to and from meeting rooms," Ryburg says. "It's much easier to just store things for later meetings."

William Miller, director of research and business development for Steelcase, the office-furniture manufacturer based in Grand Rapids, Michigan, emphasizes that mobility is about more than convenience. The radical redesign of work, he argues, requires a radical redesign of meeting space.

"Knowledge workers spend 80% of their time at the office away from their desks," Miller says. "Where are they? Working on projects. The way to support that work is to build project clusters and co-locate desks around them. You can post information and never take it down. We call it 'information persistence.' And we don't talk about meetings. We talk about 'interactions.' It's part of the new science of effective work."

*Sin #7: Meetings never get better.* People make the same mistakes.
*Salvation:* Practice makes perfect. Monitor what works and what doesn't and hold people accountable.

Meetings are like any other part of business life: you get better only if you commit to it—and aim high. Charles Schwab & Co., the financial-services company based in San Francisco, has made that commitment. In virtually every meeting at Schwab, someone serves as an "observer" and creates what the company calls a Plus/Delta list. The list records what went right and what went wrong, and gets included in the minutes. Over time, both for specific meeting groups and for the company as a whole, these lists create an agenda for change.

How much can meetings improve? The last word goes to Bernard DeKoven: "People don't have good meetings because they don't know what good meetings are like. Good meetings aren't just about work. They're about fun—keeping people charged up. It's more than collaboration, it's 'coliberation'—people freeing each other up to think more creatively."

# ARE YOU A MEETING MARVEL?

*A SELF-TEST FOR MEETING PARTICIPANTS*

*Directions:* Place a check mark to the left of any item that you *consistently demonstrate*. Be tough on yourself. It will help you improve

## Before the Meeting

1. ____ Offer suggestions for agenda items.

2. ____ Review the agenda.

3. ____ Read the meeting documents.

4. ____ Prepare my presentation (if required).

5. ____ Think about the key issues to be considered at the meeting.

6. ____ Gather information about the key issues to be considered.

7. ____ Talk to the leader or others about issues I don't fully understand.

8. ____ Inform the leader if I must arrive late or leave early.

9. ____ If unable to attend, inform the leader as soon as possible.

10. ____ If unable to attend, provide the leader with any action items that are due.

11. ____ If unable to attend, locate and orient a substitute (if appropriate).

## During the Meeting

12. ____ Arrive, call in, or log on before the scheduled start of the meeting.

13. ____ Actively listen to all points of view.

14. ____ Ask clear, brief questions for clarification.

15. ___ Offer my opinion in a clear and straightforward manner.

16. ___ Share my expertise in a way that furthers the meeting's objectives.

17. ___ Challenge assumptions but stay constructive and on topic.

18. ___ Be open to new ideas, facts, data, and methodologies.

19. ___ Help the leader stay on time and on topic.

20. ___ Seek the participation of others.

21. ___ Stay focused on the topic at hand.

22. ___ Refrain from monopolizing the discussion, being unnecessarily argumentative, engaging in side conversation, or any other dysfunctional behavior.

23. ___ Take notes, especially on key decisions and action items.

24. ___ Turn off my cell phone, beeper, and other electronic devices.

25. ___ Help the leader reach a consensus on key decisions.

26. ___ Help the leader harmonize conflict and resolve differences productively.

27. ___ Treat other team members with respect.

## After the Meeting

28. ___ Report key decisions and other information to my department.

29. ___ Begin work on my action items.

30. ___ Provide feedback on the meeting to the team leader (as appropriate).

31. ___ Communicate with other team members on joint issues and concerns.

## Self-Scoring

26–31    You are a Meeting Marvel . . . a candidate for the Meeting Hall of Fame. Keep up the good work! But don't stop trying to get better. There's always the possibility of being a player on the new reality television show, "The Facilitator."

20–25    You're not Captain Marvel yet but you're not a Meeting Monster either. So review the list of items again and keep doing the positive things while you expand your meeting repertoire and skill set.

Below 25    Go directly to Meeting Jail. You are badly in need of immediate rehabilitation, intensive training, and long-term attitude adjustment. If you do not change, the Meeting Hall of Shame awaits you!

## Marvelous Improvement Plan

List here three things you will do to become a Meeting Marvel.

1. _____

_____

2. _____

_____

3. _____

_____

# RESOURCE D

## WHAT WOULD YOU DO?

*PROBLEM SITUATIONS FOR MEETING FACILITATORS*

Review the following situations and decide what you would do to address and correct the problem. Refer to the tools listed as resources for additional ideas on how to handle the situation.

### 1. Late Start

The meeting notice and agenda was sent to members 72 hours in advance of the meeting. The notice stated that the meeting will be held Tuesday and begin at 8:30 A.M.

It is now Tuesday at 8:45 A.M. At this time, besides you (the facilitator), two other members are in the meeting room. The team consists of a total of 12 members.

What would you do?

---

**Related Tools**

#7: Establishing Your Team's Ground Rules

#10: Your Opening Act

#12: Meeting Time Management

---

### 2. Off Track

About midway through the videoconference, two members get into a heated discussion about a very specific issue concerning the market potential of two rival products. The topic being discussed is not on the agenda but is relevant to the overall team mission and may be important at a later stage of the project. The other eight members at the meeting (located in two different sites) look bored.

What would you do?

---

### Related Tools

#13: Staying on Track

#16: Communicating in a Videoconference

---

## 3. Multi-Tasking Member

One member of the team continuously works at her laptop during the course of the meeting. She appears to be responding to e-mail messages while other members are talking. She rarely asks questions or in other ways participates in team discussions. This behavior has persisted for at least the past four meetings. However, when she provides updates on her aspects of the project and reports on her action items, the work is always of high quality and on time.

What would you do?

---

### Related Tools

#7: Establishing Your Team's Ground Rules

#23: Managing Meeting Monsters

---

## 4. Rush to the Door

You are finishing up a three-hour project team meeting about 15 minutes late. As the last agenda item is completed, people begin to gather their materials and stand up ready to leave. You want to establish the norm of evaluating each meeting. Now is the time to do it but you are concerned that people may not have the patience to stay around any longer.

What would you do?

---

**Related Tools**

#26: Ending Meetings On Time and On Target

#27: Meeting Evaluation: A Two-Minute Drill

---

## 5. The Silent Majority

Your team is composed of 10 members, 4 of whom are based in the United States while the remaining 6 are from various countries in Europe. During teleconferences you have noticed that when the U.S. members present ideas or ask questions, the members from Europe rarely respond. The only time the European members will participate is when a colleague from Europe asks a question or presents a report.

What would you do?

---

**Related Tool**

#18: Achieving Clear Communication in a Multicultural Meeting

---

## 6. Progress Process

Your team meetings typically consist of progress updates by the members, who each discourse on their own aspect of the project. Members are very good about preparing for the meetings including sending slides and other materials out to the other members well in advance of the meeting. However, you are concerned because little or no discussion follows any of the progress reports.

What would you do?

---

**Related Tools**

#7: Establishing Your Team's Ground Rules

#14: How to Get Effective Participation

---

## 7. Shouting Match

Your project team has been in existence for more than two years. You have made great progress and your team is highly regarded by senior management. However, a recent development has caused some contention between two key members. During the current meeting when the team gets to this issue on the agenda, a discussion of possible options escalates into a loud two-sided argument. The other members are sitting quietly but their nonverbal behavior indicates they are very uncomfortable with the situation.

What would you do?

---

**Related Tools**

#21: Resolving Conflicts in a Team Meeting

#23: Managing Meeting Monsters

---

## 8. Bored Meeting

This is now the third meeting where the overall energy level among members is low. There is very little discussion, no reactions to reports, and minimal responses to questions. Your informal survey reveals that members are bored and do not enjoy the meetings. They describe the meetings as "dull" and "uninteresting." The team still has important work to do, so the problem is not with the task but rather with the process side of the meetings.

What would you do?

---

**Related Tools**

#14: How to Get Effective Participation

#24: Serious Fun at Team Meetings? You're Kidding!

---

## 9. Decision Revision

Your team seems to be well run. It has an agenda for all meetings, and it has developed a set of norms and is making progress on its project plan. Its members have also made a series of important project decisions. Unfortunately, they tend to revisit decisions made in previous meetings. This is frustrating because a decision appears to be made at a meeting; it gets recorded in the meeting notes, and none of the members object to it when they see it in the notes. However, at the next meeting, someone will bring up the very same issue and want to debate it again, and everyone returns to the fray. This has happened several times in the last six months.

What would you do?

---

**Related Tools**

#13: Staying on Track

#19: How to Make a Decision

#30: Meeting Notes

#32: After-Meeting Actions

---

## 10. Tedious Talk

Once again a member is delivering a presentation that seems to be going on and on. The slide count is probably passing 50, including many slides that are difficult to read because of the small font. Members are alternatively bored and confused. And yet the topic and information in the presentation is important for the team to understand because it will be needed in the next phase of the project. You know members have questions about the issue but none are forthcoming.

What would you do?

---

**Related Tools**

#12: Meeting Time Management

#20: Presenting at a Team Meeting

#23: Managing Meeting Monsters

---

# RESOURCE E

## MEETING EXCELLENCE

### YOUR FINAL EXAM

## *Purpose*

The purpose of this tool is to provide a review of some of the key elements of *Meeting Excellence.* How much do you know about effective meeting planning and facilitation?

*Directions.* Review each item. Circle or check your answer. Then see the "Answer Clues" for ideas on where to find the answer and more information on the issue.

1. In preparing your meeting agenda, always:

_____ (a) List the key meeting outcome as the first item on the agenda to ensure that it will receive the time and attention it deserves.

_____ (b) Ensure that all items are allocated an equal amount of time.

_____ (c) List the key meeting outcome as second or third item so that people who arrive late will have a chance to participate in the discussion.

_____ (d) Start with administrative items so you can get them out of the way before discussion begins on the important issues.

_____ (e) Only a and b above.

_____ (f) None of the above.

2. Your agenda should include a time estimate for each item:

_____ (a) That can be changed if more time is needed to resolve the issue.

_____ (b) To estimate the total amount of time needed for the meeting.

_____ (c) Because it helps to control the discussion at a meeting.

_____ (d) To help the people responsible for each item to plan their presentation and discussion.

_____ (e) All of the above.

_____ (f) None of the above.

3. Your agenda should be sent out to members:

_____ (a) At least 24 hours prior to the meeting.

_____ (b) At least 48 hours prior to the meeting.

_____ (c) At the time established in the team norms.

_____ (d) At the time established by senior management.

_____ (e) Both b and c above.

_____ (f) None of the above.

4. As the facilitator of a videoconference, you should:

_____ (a) Change your seat frequently in order to see everyone and so everyone can see you.

_____ (b) Arrive early to make sure the equipment is up and running.

_____ (c) Wear bright patterns that can be easily seen by people at the other sites.

_____ (d) Avoid reacting to nonverbal actions of people in other sites because they can be difficult to interpret in a video screen.

_____ (e) All of the above.

_____ (f) None of the above.

5.  In a teleconference:

    _____ (a) Do not multi-task (do other work during the meeting).

    _____ (b) Try not to call in on a cell phone.

    _____ (c) Identify yourself at the beginning of the meeting.

    _____ (d) Let the other person finish before you speak.

    _____ (e) All of the above.

    _____ (f) Both c and d above.

6.  As a facilitator, the most important thing you can say at the opening of a meeting is:

    _____ (a) The purpose or key outcome of the meeting.

    _____ (b) Welcome the group and thank them for attending.

    _____ (c) Review the relevant norms.

    _____ (d) Identify a person to take the meeting notes.

    _____ (e) Both b and c above.

    _____ (f) None of the above.

7.  As a facilitator, the most important thing you can do to close a meeting is:

    _____ (a) Thank the group for their hard work.

    _____ (b) Indicate the day, time, and location of the next meeting.

    _____ (c) Evaluate the effectiveness of the meeting.

    _____ (d) Summarize the key decisions made at the meeting.

    _____ (e) Both a and c above.

    _____ (f) None of the above.

8. As a facilitator, you should consider canceling your meeting if:

_____ (a) No conference rooms are available.

_____ (b) Information needed for a critical decision is not available.

_____ (c) The agenda only includes reports by members.

_____ (d) Members complain about too many meetings.

_____ (e) Only b and c above.

_____ (f) None of the above.

9. Every action item should include:

_____ (a) The subject of the item.

_____ (b) The action required.

_____ (c) The person responsible for the item.

_____ (d) The date the item is due.

_____ (e) All of the above.

_____ (f) Only a and d above.

10. As a facilitator, if you are concerned about getting action on a key action item, the best thing you can do is:

_____ (a) Do the work yourself.

_____ (b) Hire a temporary worker or contractor to do the work.

_____ (c) Remind the person responsible for the item prior to the due date.

_____ (d) Send a copy of the action item list to the person's manager.

_____ (e) All of the above.

_____ (f) None of the above.

11. As a team member, building and maintaining the trust of your teammates usually involves:

_____ (a) Only making commitments that you honestly expect to
deliver.

_____ (b) Speaking openly, honestly, and directly with the team
leader if you have a complaint about the performance of a
teammate.

_____ (c) Informing everyone if you make a mistake, find you made
an error in judgment, or are unable to complete an action item
on time.

_____ (d) Working exclusively within your area of subject matter
expertise so as not to insult and devalue the expertise of your
teammates.

_____ (e) Only a and c above.

_____ (f) All of the above.

12. As a facilitator, you can build trust with members of your team by:

_____ (a) Confronting them directly in a meeting when they make a
mistake.

_____ (b) Empowering them to make decisions or take action on
behalf of the team.

_____ (c) Asking them what is causing the problem when they are
having difficulties honoring their commitments to the team.

_____ (d) Speaking directly to the person's manager when they, for
example, are having problems understanding the issues or
getting the work done on time.

_____ (e) All of the above.

_____ (f) None of the above.

13. During a meeting when a small number of people are having an in-depth discussion while the rest of the team is bored and uninvolved, the facilitator should:

_____ (a) Ask the small group to conclude their discussion on an interim basis in the next five minutes.

_____ (b) Ask the small group to form a subteam that meets after the meeting to discuss and, if necessary, resolve the issue.

_____ (c) Ask the small group to take the next 15 minutes to conclude their discussion while the remainder of the team takes a break.

_____ (d) Explain the situation ("only a few members are involved") and then refer the issue to the parking lot for discussion, if time permits, at the end of the meeting, as a possible agenda item at the next meeting, or as the topic for consideration by a subteam.

_____ (e) Any of the above.

_____ (f) None of the above.

14. When considering the best time to hold a team meeting, you should think about meeting:

_____ (a) Monday morning to get the week off to a good start and allow time for action items to be completed during the rest of the week.

_____ (b) Friday afternoon because participants will not want to have long discussions that extend the meeting late in the day.

_____ (c) Right after lunch when people have renewed energy from the intake of food.

_____ (d) Very early in the morning so that the participants can complete the meeting and still have the most of the rest of the day to complete their other tasks.

_____ (e) Both a and b above.

_____ (f) None of the above.

15. A general guideline for taking a break during a meeting is:

_____ (a) Take a break after a minimum of two hours of meeting time.

_____ (b) A break should last at least 20 minutes to allow people enough time to get refreshed and reenergized.

_____ (c) No meeting should go longer than 90 minutes without a break.

_____ (d) Allow any member to call a break if it looks like the group energy is low, people need to use the rest rooms, or the meeting has gone on for too long.

_____ (e) Only a and b above.

_____ (f) Only c and d above.

16. As a facilitator, one thing you should *not* do when trying to integrate a new member is:

_____ (a) Get together immediately to talk about the goals of the team and their role on the team.

_____ (b) Provide the person with the team charter, project plan, norms, recent meeting notes, and any other relevant documents as soon as possible.

_____ (c) Wait several meetings before giving the person an action item or other task so they can get comfortable with how the team works.

_____ (d) Assign a current member to serve as the person's mentor and adviser so you do not have to do it.

_____ (e) None of the above.

17. As a facilitator, when a member leaves the team, it is important that you:

_____ (a) Conduct an exit interview to collect the departing member's perceptions of the effectiveness of the team and ways the team needs to improve.

_____ (b) Ask the person to stop attending team meetings immediately because they will no longer be interested in the work of the team and may have a negative influence on the climate of meetings.

_____ (c) Speak with departing member's manager to have some influence on the selection of the person's replacement.

_____ (d) Ensure that the departing member not speak with the incoming member in order to allow the new person the freedom to develop a fresh perception of the team.

_____ (e) All of the above.

_____ (f) Only a and c above.

_____ (g) None of the above.

18. Before you confront a member who consistently exhibits dysfunctional behavior in your meetings, you should:

_____ (a) Consider the consequences of doing nothing and allowing the behavior to continue.

_____ (b) Have a clear plan as to how you will approach the person.

_____ (c) Remember to focus only on the person's behavior that you have observed in your meetings.

_____ (d) Allow the person the opportunity to respond to your statement of the situation.

_____ (e) All of the above.

_____ (f) Only b and c above.

_____ (g) None of the above.

19. One of the best ways to minimize the impact of dysfunctional behavior on your team meetings is to:

    _____ (a) Confront the person directly in the meeting the first time you observe negative behavior.

    _____ (b) During the forming stage, establish a clear set of behavioral norms for team meetings.

    _____ (c) Meet with the person's manager as soon as possible after the meeting in which you observed the dysfunctional actions.

    _____ (d) If the negative behavior continues over time, ask another team member who knows the person well to discuss it with him or her.

    _____ (e) All of the above.

    _____ (f) None of the above.

20. A good reason for a team to develop a plan to communicate with key stakeholders outside of the team is to:

    _____ (a) Obtain resources needed to support the team's objectives.

    _____ (b) Get them to clear away any obstacles that may stand in the way of team success.

    _____ (c) Solicit ideas and suggestions for solving team problems or addressing other issues.

    _____ (d) Reduce the amount and degree of outside interference in the ongoing work of your team.

    _____ (e) Only a and d above.

    _____ (f) All of the above.

    _____ (g) None of the above.

21. The four most important team roles are:

_____ (a) Leader, facilitator, scribe, and timekeeper.

_____ (b) Facilitator, scribe, timekeeper, and parking lot attendant.

_____ (c) Leader, facilitator, meeting participant, and timekeeper.

_____ (d) Leader, facilitator, scribe, and meeting participant.

_____ (e) None of the above.

22. At a new team kick-off meeting, people most often forget to:

_____ (a) Invite the senior management sponsor to address the group.

_____ (b) Ask members to share their concerns and questions about the team.

_____ (c) Present an overview of the project.

_____ (d) Begin the process of developing a team charter.

_____ (e) None of the above.

_____ (f) Only a and d above.

23. Having fun in a team meeting can help your team succeed by:

_____ (a) Creating an informal and relaxed climate.

_____ (b) Helping to create a climate of trust and open communication.

_____ (c) Establishing an atmosphere where more effective problem solving and decision making takes place.

_____ (d) Encouraging people to be more creative and innovative in their thinking.

_____ (e) All of the above.

_____ (f) None of the above.

24. If your primary language is English, one of the worst things you can do when you communicate with someone whose primary language is not English is:

____ (a) Speak slowly because people may find it insulting.

____ (b) Avoid colloquial expressions.

____ (c) Use sports analogies and slang in an effort to create a bond with the other person.

____ (d) Practice active listening because people may find it annoying to have their ideas repeated back to them.

____ (e) None of the above.

____ (f) All of the above.

25. When planning an off-site meeting for your team, ensure that:

____ (a) The group has a clear reason to meet.

____ (b) You have a structured agenda similar to a regular team meeting.

____ (c) The meeting location is consistent with the meeting's objectives.

____ (d) The team completes all the work it begins during the off-site meeting because getting people to do follow-up work is unlikely.

____ (e) Only a and c above.

____ (f) All of the above.

## FINAL EXAM ANSWER CLUES

1. See tool #3: How to Prepare an Action Agenda

2. See tool #3: How to Prepare an Action Agenda

3. See tool #2: Preparing for Your Next Meeting

4. See tool #16: Communicating in a Videoconference

5. See tool #17: Teleconference Tips

6. See tool #10: Your Opening Act

7. See tool #25: Ending Meetings On Time and On Target

8. See tool #1: Is This Meeting Necessary?

9. See tool #31: Getting Action on Action Items

10. See tool #31: Getting Action on Action Items

11. See tool #15: Building a Foundation of Trust

12. See tool #15: Building a Foundation of Trust

13. See tool #13: Staying on Track

14. See tool #12: Meeting Time Management

15. See tool #12: Meeting Time Management

16. See tool #5: How to Integrate a New Member

17. See tool #6: When a Member Leaves the Team

18. See tool #23: Managing Meeting Monsters

19. See tool #23: Managing Meeting Monsters

20. See tool #33: Managing External Communications

21. See tool #4: Defining Team Meeting Roles

22. See tool #8: Components of a New Team Kick-Off Meeting

23. See tool #24: Serious Fun at Team Meetings? You're Kidding!

24. See tool #18: Achieving Clear Communication in a Multicultural Meeting

25. See tool #9: Planning an Off-Site Meeting That's On Target

# RESOURCE F

## ANNOTATED BIBLIOGRAPHY OF MEETING RESOURCES

This bibliography is not intended to be an exhaustive list of all available resources on meetings. You will find many more books and articles on meetings, for example, than we have cited here. We have attempted here to present a sampling of the resources that we have found to be especially useful in our work.

### Books

Mosvick, R. K., & Nelson, R. B. *A Guide to Successful Meeting Management.* Indianapolis, Ind.: Park Avenue, 1996.

> A very good source of data on the state of meetings in business, including how people spend their time and the high level of dissatisfaction with the quality of meetings. It also includes suggestions for improving meeting effectiveness.

Silberman, M. *101 Ways to Make Your Meetings Active.* San Francisco: Jossey-Bass/Pfeiffer, 1999.

> The best resource for exercises and fun activities to train people in effective meeting process.

Kieffer, G. D. *The Strategy of Meetings.* New York: Simon & Schuster, 1988.

> A very thoughtful book on the psychology of meetings and how to prepare yourself mentally for a successful meeting.

Doyle, M., & Strauss, D. *How to Make Meetings Work.* Chicago: Playboy Press, 1976.

> A modern-day classic, this book is full of principles that still apply today, especially the five ingredients of a successful meeting: focus on process, content, open communication, protecting people from attack, and clear roles. It does not cover current meeting dilemmas such as virtual meetings and global teams.

Streibel, B. J. *The Manager's Guide to Effective Meetings.* New York: McGraw-Hill, 2003.

> As a more recent publication, this book touches on current issues such as teleconferences and videoconferences (but not global meetings) in an effective way. It also includes some good checklists and examples.

## Articles

Mankins, M. "Stop Wasting Valuable Time." *Harvard Business Review,* Sept. 2004, pp. 58–65.

> This article is valuable because it focuses on executive team meetings, an area often overlooked in the literature. The value of the article lies in the seven recommendations that will stop wasting the valuable meeting time of executives.

Burns, G. "The Secrets of Team Facilitation." *Training & Development,* June 1995, pp. 46–52.

> While they are not really secrets, Burns's eight "domains of knowledge" are important tools in understanding the requirements for being an effective meeting facilitator. The list could be helpful in creating a facilitator assessment tool and providing the basis for facilitator training.

Rangarajan, N., & Rohrbaugh, J. "Multiple Roles on Online Facilitation: An Example of Any-Time, Any-Place Meetings." *Group Facilitation,* Spring 2003, pp. 26–37.

This article is a useful supplement to the Burns article for its study of eight facilitator roles in Web-based meetings of geographically dispersed teams. One important conclusion of this study was that the use of a facilitator was quite helpful to the meeting process but less useful when it came to resolving conflict and generating a true consensus.

Prewitt, E. "Pitfalls in Meetings and How to Avoid Them. *Harvard Management Update,* June 1998, pp. 3–5.

A solid summary article on the seven pitfalls and some tips on how to address them. The seven pitfalls include some areas that are rarely covered in the literature, such as overdeveloped egos, goals that could be better accomplished by other means, and jumping to conclusions.

Krattenmaker, T. "Before and After the Meeting." *Harvard Management Communication Letter,* Oct. 2000, pp. 3–5.

A good reminder that the success of your meeting is best determined by what you do both to prepare for and to follow up on the meeting.

## Web Sites

3M Meeting Network, *www.3M.com/meetingnetwork/*.

The granddaddy of meeting Web sites and still the best. It contains wonderful short articles, tips from experts, book reviews, an advice column, and even cartoons. Sadly, we must report that the future of this site is in doubt as 3M has halted updates and may elect to take the site down at some point in the future.

Your Meeting Resource Center, *www.effectivemeetings.com*.

A close runner-up, this site contains many good short pieces on meeting planning, facilitation, and technology, including some offbeat tools such as the meeting "cost calculator."

Live Meeting, *www.microsoft.com*.

Click on Live Meeting for information on a free trial, to participate in a live demo, and other information about this online meeting resource.

Trainers Warehouse, *www.trainerswarehouse.com*.

A great resource for hundreds of serious and fun products to improve both the quality and climate of your next meeting.

## Videos

CRM Learning, *Meeting Robbers*. Revised Edition, Carlsbad, Calif.: CRM Learning, undated.

This humorous 21-minute video is built around a team of "meeting monsters" who do their best to disrupt a meeting. The meeting facilitator demonstrates how to handle difficult behavior in the next meeting as well as effective actions outside the meeting that contribute to meeting excellence.

Kantola Productions, *Be Prepared for Meetings*. Mill Valley, Calif.: Kantola Productions, undated.

In just 21 minutes this straightforward, no-nonsense video reviews the essentials of preparing for and facilitating a problem-solving business meeting. The focus is on important tools such as starting on time, reviewing the key outcomes, staying on track, and closing with a solid summary of actions and next steps.

# ABOUT THE AUTHORS

**Glenn Parker** works with organizations to create and sustain high-performing teams, effective team players, and team-based systems. His best-selling book, *Team Players and Teamwork* (Jossey-Bass, 1990), was selected as one of the 10 best business books its year. Now in its seventh printing, it has been published in several other languages. Glenn is the author of some 15 other books, facilitator guides, and instruments, including the recently revised update of his best-seller, *Cross-Functional Teams* (Jossey-Bass, 2003) and the widely used instrument, the *Parker Team Player Survey* (CPP, 1992). Glenn is one of only 75 management experts recognized in *The Guru Guide* (Wiley, 1998).

Glenn is a hands-on consultant and trainer who works with start-up and ongoing teams of all types in a variety of industries. He facilitates team building, conducts training workshops, consults with management, and gives presentations for organizations across a wide variety of industries. His clients have included pharmaceutical companies such as Novartis, Merck and Company, Johnson & Johnson, and Bristol-Myers Squibb; a variety of industrial organizations such as 3M, Kimberly-Clark, The Budd Company, Penntech Papers, AlliedSignal, and Sun MicroSystems; companies in telecommunications including AT&T, Pacific Bell, NYNEX, and Lucent/Bell Labs; service businesses such as Commerce Clearing House's Legal Information Service, Asea Brown Boveri (ABB) Environmental Services, American Express, and the *New England Journal of Medicine,* and many others, as well as teams from government agencies at the EPA, NIH, Department of the Navy, and the U.S. Coast Guard.

Glenn holds a B.A. from City College of New York, an M.A. from the University of Illinois, and has studied for the doctorate at Cornell University. He is much in demand as a speaker at corporate meetings and at international professional conferences in human resources, team development, and project management.

Glenn is the father of three grown children and lives with his wife, Judy, in central New Jersey. In his spare time, he volunteers with the American Cancer

Society, roots for the Philadelphia 76ers, rides his bike, and plans his next vacation. For more information: www.glennparker.com.

**Robert Hoffman** is currently working as executive director of organizational development for Novartis Oncology. In this role, he provides coaching and guidance to global managers and team leaders in one of Novartis's leading businesses. He works with teams, groups, and individuals to jointly develop solutions and responses to team performance issues, organizational change projects, and individual and managerial development needs.

Bob has been with Novartis since 2001, starting in the research and development organization. Prior to joining Novartis, Bob spent 12 years with Warner-Lambert, which he joined in 1988 as corporate training manager. He progressed through several corporate HR positions and moved to the Parke-Davis division in 1994. He supported the U.S. Sales and Marketing organizations and was ultimately asked to join the "Go-To-Market" project on a full-time basis, helping Parke-Davis adopt key learnings from its successful launch of Lipitor, the world's largest-selling pharmaceutical product.

Building on this success, Bob relocated to Ann Arbor, Michigan, to provide organizational development support for the Parke-Davis R&D group. When Warner-Lambert was acquired by Pfizer, Bob was one of four people chosen in Ann Arbor to provide full-time support to the integration activities. These activities were widely seen as best practice and were documented extensively in the press and academic literature.

Bob has also worked in Human Resources in the banking, retailing, and publishing industries. He received his master's degree in industrial psychology from the University of Akron in 1982. Additionally, Bob was one of the first participants in a unique doctoral program offered by George Washington University, in which participants attended the program full time while still employed. Bob started this program in 1992 and successfully completed his dissertation in the area of career development in 1997.

Bob resides in Watchung, New Jersey, with his wife, Deanna, and their four children.

# INDEX